In His Image

Gene & Beulah,

The two of you are wonderful examples of the way God wants us to use the talents He has given each of us. Your creative and active lives mirror God's own, which is what He has told us to do in serving Him and your fellowmen.

Robert G. Horn

You are precious friends.

Bob

In His Image

Cover design: Sandra Horn

For information:
hornrg@hotmail.com

Editor's Note

It's a pleasure to commend to you the writing and thoughts of Dr. Robert Horn. I have no doubt you will be stimulated to contemplation and discourse as he shares his ideas. Rooted solidly in the Christian faith and a conviction of American ideals, this book is meant to stir each reader to stronger faith and a life that makes the difference God intends. God bless you as you read, think, reflect, and take action!

Michael W. Newman

Contents

Preface

In His Image

Entrepreneurial behavior and American Exceptionalism are popular study and discussion topics, especially as they relate to free enterprise, freedom's offspring. Both are crucial elements of the pursuit for a return to global economic leadership. In a surprising twist that goes well beyond business prowess, however, the narrative of this book uncovers a realization that this energizing capacity resides in each of us and permeates every aspect of life. As told in the Genesis creation story, the image of God is inborn in every person, which renders all humans exceptional, not just Americans. This matchless gift endows each of us with God's character traits: knowledge, understanding, and wisdom. Yet, this extraordinary capacity is not given to us for self-centered purposes. We are privileged and empowered in a partnership with our Maker to use our entrepreneurial creativity and initiative to subdue and have dominion over creation by serving God and our fellowman.

This capability isn't new. God hasn't changed, neither His Word nor His purpose. The Gospel's good news has always spoken truth to power and freedom. It is people who are fraudulent and fickle, constantly shifting, insecure, and erratic. Our short attention span can make the life and story of Jesus, once fresh and penetrating, seem old and outdated. Like a blanket of lethargy, apathy smothers God's revolutionary and right side up reality. The laziness of mankind is very much like that of the servant with one talent, recorded in Jesus' parable of the talents (Matthew 25: 14-30). Perhaps it is part of the reason membership in the Christian Church has been steadily declining for over fifty years. Christian and non-Christian, we all need to hear the recreating and renewing good news the way it was received by those who first heard it. God's Word has not changed, but new ways to convey its unchanging message can reawaken mankind to its ageless truth and hope that make us heirs, sons and daughters of the King.

The way of the serpent, defined in Chapter 1, entices us with the temptation that we can be like God, knowing good and evil. What mankind learned too late is that the "good" promised in the garden is merely lust for what we desire. "Evil" is no more than an aversion to what we fear. The free will choice of mankind to this ultimate either/or decision not only severed the interpersonal bond between God and humans, it also relegated mankind to an every person for herself or himself survival of the fittest. The final outcome is not pretty. It dooms those who remain under the serpent's sway to eternal separation from God. The weeping and gnashing of teeth talked about in Scripture may best be understood as wild beasts fighting ravenously over a dead animal carcass, provoked purely by greed and selfishness.

Yet, God did not abandon humanity. He sent a second, or last Adam, who held to the promise of inheritance as the Son of the King. The death penalty pronounced on mankind for rejecting God was received and satisfied by the last Adam. His deliberate step into the breach between God and judgment not only paid a blood ransom for our rescue from sin, it also enabled a return to an interpersonal relationship between God and every person, just as it was in the beginning.

Finally, this book is not a training manual. The image of God that resides in each of us is unique DNA and different for every person. Each reader draws on his or her entrepreneurial capabilities, like the servants with two and five talents. Attempting to duplicate the entrepreneurial success of someone else belittles the unique talent (or talents) each of us has received from the Creator. Be yourself; everyone else is already taken. *"Well done, good and faithful servant! You have been faithful with a few things; I will put you in charge of many things. Come and enjoy your Master's happiness!" (Matthew 25:21 NIV)*

RGH

Prologue

*"The highest heavens belong to the Lord, but the
earth He has given to man" (Psalm 115:16 NIV)*

Nothing. Black on black. The Spirit hovers over a deep
and formless void and a voice echoes, *"Let there be light."
(Genesis 1:3 NIV)* The Creator reveals Himself. From utter
nothingness God generates something-ness. This act of faith
exerts creative energy to make what is not. *"Now faith is being
sure of what we hope for and certain of what we do not see"
(Hebrews 11:1 (NIV).* His Word crafts the enormity and
intricacy of the entire universe, all universes.

To complete His handiwork, God forms humans from
dirt. Male and female are created in His image so they may
emulate His creativity. God's focus is on them, partners in His
new adventure in a new world. They are the reason for creation.
Maybe you have read Genesis 1 so often that it seems
unremarkable. It is anything but ordinary. Watch the "replay" as
God, one knee on the ground, shapes the crown of His creation
and leans over to breathe life directly into the nostrils. Picture the
anticipation as His arms cradle the inert body. See His delight
when this final creation breathes independently and opened eyes
see God's countenance for the first time. Was God's expression
like Thomas Edison's when the light bulb finally worked or
Steven Jobs' at an Apple product launch? It is the other way
around. The faces of Edison and Jobs mirrored the Creator's.

Fast forward: September 11, 2001. Terrorists flew hijacked aircraft into the World Trade towers and initiated a cascade of destruction and death, wreaking evil havoc. You may recall your exact location when you heard the news. Shocking pictures of the attacks and aftermath permanently etch our memories. Images of first responders amidst dead, wounded, and stunned victims in clouds of choking gray dust from pulverized cement and steel are not easily deleted.

How did it go from majesty and splendor to wreckage and ruin? This wasn't the worst man-made tragedy ever. Imagine the news lead on September 17, 1862, had there been television. "During the first hours of the Battle of Antietam close to 10,000 Union and Rebel soldiers were killed, stacked like cordwood!" It stuns the hardest person. In 1862, however, news travelled slowly, not reaching many for months. The 9/11 attacks played out like a reality show. Across the U.S. we watched, riveted to TV screens as the devastation unfolded. Is this still the land of the free and home of the brave, welcoming all who seek refuge and a better life? Has America changed?

The initial intent of this book was to propose that free enterprise can be revitalized by returning to the entrepreneurial DNA that has built and nourished it since the American Revolution. That is still a goal, but as entrepreneurial origins were probed it became clear that there is a greater force shaping our world than the mindset of genius inventors and business innovators. It led back to the Genesis creation narrative and the Master Entrepreneur. There is more. Being created in the image of God, all humans received this attribute. A powerful vestige still resides in all of us. God still wishes to partner with us. He tells us how and where in His directive to *"...subdue and have dominion over" (Genesis 1:28 NIV)* creation. Far beyond inspiring a renewal of free enterprise, it enriches all facets of our lives: spiritual, physiological, moral, intellectual, social, and political as well as economic.

The book highlights and contrasts opposing belief systems and related behaviors. The first is the Way of the Lord. It represents the interpersonal relationship God pursues with each of us. Its character traits are faith and action, motivated by faith and driven by the Spirit. In the talents parable the Master imparts knowledge, understanding, and wisdom to all three servants so they are equipped to carry out his directive. *"The Spirit of the Lord will rest on Him – the Spirit of wisdom and of understanding, the Spirit of counsel and of power, the Spirit of knowledge and the fear of the Lord" (Isaiah 11:2 NIV)*. This is the image of God bestowed at creation, after which He charges humans to take care of His handiwork. Jesus clarifies and explicates the Creator's charge with His answer to the cynical lawyer: *"Love the Lord your God with all your heart and with all your soul and with all your mind...And...Love your neighbor as yourself" (Matthew 22:37-40 NIV)*. That's the entire Law of God. Serve God and our fellowman. Oh, please note that there is no precept to serve self.

Talents represent personhood. Each of us has received a unique DNA fingerprint. Don't emulate someone else's life. The Creator gave you a separate identity and an exclusive charge to use your talents to subdue and have dominion. It applies to all, whether we have one, two, or five talents. The servants with five and two talents served God and fellowman, not themselves. *"...do not worry about your life, what you will eat or drink; or about your body, what you will wear...Who of you by worrying can add a single hour to his life?...seek first His kingdom and His righteousness, and all these things will be given to you as* well" (Matthew 6:25-34 NIV). Faith and action spring from attitudes instilled by the Master when He gave us His own image.

The way of the serpent, led by Satan, abhors faith and the action it motivates. The parables of the rich fool and the talents expose its darkness. The rich fool, certain that success is his own doing, compounds his flawed logic by hoarding. Judgment is as stark as it is unexpected: *"You fool! This very night your life will be demanded from you"* (Luke 12:20 NIV). The servant with one talent expects others to satisfy his needs and desires. Laziness and indifference bring judgment and separation from the Master. *"You wicked, lazy servant...take the bag of gold from him and give it to the one who has ten bags...throw that worthless servant outside, into the darkness, where there will be weeping and gnashing of teeth."* (Matthew 25:26-30 NIV) The rich fool and the lazy servant share motives and attitudes of self-service that ignore God and others. Judgment is not a calculation of wealth, honors, and recognition. Separation from God is self-inflicted. It results from an attitude that trusts and serves only self.

The writer is unapologetically Christian and patriotic. Millions share these values. The Creator seeks the partnership of us all in this exciting venture. We know the rest of the story and we all need to be a part of it. The prayer is that this book will help uncover the entrepreneurial capacity you have received and stir you to serve God and your fellowmen.

Chapter One

Subdue and Have Dominion

On Course

Why didn't God just eradicate the faithless creation and be done with it? Instead, He stayed on course. He didn't let the serpent's treachery, human infidelity, or anything else disrupt His plan.

It is no surprise. *"I the Lord do not change" (Malachi 3:6 NIV)*. From the beginning, His intent and desire has been an interpersonal bond with each of us. This is obviously of great importance, for He sent His Son as a blood ransom to put our relationship with Him back on track. It makes no sense. After all, we are contemptible and actively resist reconciliation. Surely, God can do better. He's perfect. We're the opposite. We focus on self, the essence of our attempt to be god. Our thinking is upside down. It doesn't work. It is impossible to escape sin by striving to avoid it. *"...our righteous acts are like filthy rags" (Isaiah 64:6 NIV)*. Our perspective is out of kilter and must be changed.

The wonderful fact is God didn't abandon creation. It has nothing to do with us. God receives no counsel from humans. His reason and logic are beyond our ken. We know only what He reveals. His plan, regardless of His reasoning, is to restore His relationship with us. That relationship is the underlying purpose of creation and God won't abandon it. Neither should we. Often, injustice seems to prevail and the world's fatal flaws glare like neon. We feel discouraged and persecuted, tempted to cease efforts to make a difference. Why not abandon everything, and wait for Jesus to return? Some have, but it is just another self-centered act. It certainly isn't where God leads.

God understands the toll evil takes. He knows rejection. How did He feel when the humans He created in His own image rebelled and tried to create a new reality based on lies and evil? Still, He stayed true to His purpose. He initiated a new strategy that encompassed even more rejection, more violence, and darker deeds as His Son was murdered by an unruly mob. Imagine that! God watched His own Son die a horrific death. Parents who bury a child may receive a small glimpse, but not one of us begins to grasp the cost of God's personal and total investment in mankind.

Thank God this is not the end of the story. Inside the risk of His Son's crucifixion is an unlikely and unpredictable twist. In His death, the Son satisfies the Father's requirement for righteousness and justice. The Son defeats the serpent, exactly as God said in the Garden. The serpent may be able to confuse and outwit humans, but God is a different and insurmountable foe. God holds to His purpose and holds onto us. He stays His course. His action was counterintuitive, opposite of our self-centered thinking. It was unexpected by Satan and defeated him once and for all. God's course reset the upside down world to its original right side up posture.

God's creation behavior flows through the ages to our time. His original purpose is unchanged. Each of us has received the gift of His image. It carries far beyond the realm of business. If we limit our perception of "entrepreneur" to extraordinary and exceptional mavericks of industry, we undervalue the Creator's gifts and short-change ourselves. The creative and creating essence of entrepreneurial behavior needs to be freed from this single dimension and recognized as the foundational spirit of who we are, no matter what we are or what we do. We are sons and daughters, heirs of the King of creation. His call leads us to live outside the lockstep, robotic world of mass-production, lethargic flesh, and conformist serpent. Freedom is restored. Don't waste your life trying to mimic the successes of others. Trust the gifts you have received and exert the initiative to be yourself. No one else has the talent you have received. Don't ignore or bury it. Life is new, challenging, fresh, and counterintuitive. It is filled with possibilities and opportunities. It is self-sacrificial. It is the *Way of the Lord*. Use it!

(Note: The *Way of the Lord* is a literary device used throughout the book. It represents faith in God and His Son, Christ. It is contrasted with the way of the serpent.)

Thousands of years ago, God called Abram to this life. Abram was told to leave his country, his people, his father's household, and his gods to embark on an adventure God promised would be an everlasting blessing to the world. Abram heeded God's call and took the risk. He had faith. He believed God would make something great out of nothing. He trusted God to do this, though he was a childless old man. Then God proceeded to do precisely what He promised. From Abram's lackluster and inconsequential life, He created a new nation and His chosen people. Abram was renamed Abraham to symbolize his partnership with God. We should not forget that this is also our heritage and legacy.

The constant new beginnings revealed in Scripture are God's entrepreneurial fingerprints. His DNA resides in us all. Daily, we are showered with *"...immeasurably more than all we can ask or imagine" (Ephesians 3:20 NIV)*. He empowers us with grace to continue creation with the commonplace resources around us and with our own lives – all for His glory and His goal of bringing His human creation back into relationship with Himself.

In all history and still today, God blesses mankind with knowledge, understanding, and wisdom. Extraordinary springs from ordinary. It is the way humans learned to control fire to use it for good. It is the hidden ingredient that facilitated invention of the wheel. As early as 1410, Iroquois Indians extracted Pennsylvania crude oil seeps for medicinal purposes, later to be transformed into innumerable crude oil products and benefits. It is how the light bulb was invented. It is the way a "bucket of sand" was transformed into Silicon Valley (http://enopetroleum.com /oildiscoveries.html).

This is the path to which God calls us. It is a new life and an adventure. It is a life that features tiny mustard seeds that grow to become trees and small children leading the way by faith. It is not easy, for it requires us to abandon the irresistible temptation of the serpent's lure and lie, *"...you will be like God" (Genesis 3:5 NIV)*. It is unpredictable, creative, and entirely effective. It is life in God's image. It is the Way of the Lord.

Freedom and captivity

How did we get here? Where do we go? When Adam and Eve chose themselves over God, they terminated the relationship bestowed as part of the Creator's image. The ill-advised misstep was catastrophic. It reduced human life to a material state, subject to the Tree of the Knowledge of Good and Evil, driven solely by lust and fear. How ironic. The mind of humans, part of God's image, concluded that they could manage alone. What fools! They didn't even realize they had reduced human reality to a mindless survival of the fittest.

For the most part, mankind gives itself a pass on this issue. Yet, it is not a casual thing. In the entire universe, nothing else comes close to the uniqueness and capabilities of the mind. By this gift, though we use only a small portion of its potential, we have the capacity for speech, logic, abstract thinking, imagination, and creativity. It is the source of inspiration, relationships, faith, hope, and peace. The mind is a complete outlier. Though it can be described, it can never be explained. Nor can its origin. Ambrose Bierce saw the enigma of trying to understand the human mind "due to the fact that it has nothing but itself to know itself with." More significantly, it begs a deeper question. Who is its source? Are we, or is God? This is inconvenient and annoying to those living in the way of the serpent, so they use the mind to sidestep it and simply deny God: God is dead. The serpent promotes this as a brilliant and irresistible answer. It is the perfect displacement of the sovereign Creator God. (Bierce, Ambrose. The Unabridged Devil's Dictionary. University of Georgia Press. January 3, 2002, first published in 1906 – http://www.gutenberg.org/ebooks)

Eliminating God, however, only worsens the predicament. Besides being dishonest it ignores significant information and leaves a blank that must be filled. Mankind may be rudderless, but the universe and its interlocking parts did not occur through some set of random incidents. It is antithetical to the systematic orderliness of earth and the universe. Some power, some being is in charge. So, if God doesn't rule, who does? The question isn't new.

It goes to the core of reality revealed by the serpent's lure in the Garden: *"...you will be like God."* *(Genesis 3:5 NIV)* This question is the ultimate "either/or" that each of us must face, unless we are so apathetic and lazy we allow the serpent to respond for us. We live or die by the answer.

Whittaker Chambers, an ex-communist, viewed the battle between freedom and communism as a political allegory of the war between God and Satan, the life and death struggle for human souls. His insights are valuable. Though he is best remembered for evidence and testimony in the trials of Alger Hiss, his book, Witness, is a lasting gift. It describes his tortured journey to Christian faith. The Foreword, titled "Letter to My Children," chronicles this pilgrimage. He came to realize that communism is not a new thing, but a retread of the second oldest faith. Its promise, unveiled in the Garden under the Tree of the Knowledge of Good and Evil, is the vision and alternate faith of mankind without God. It sets humans in the center of the universe, not because God created mankind in His image, but because the mind makes humans the most intelligent of the animals. Humans declare themselves supreme by the seemingly simple act of denying God.

Chambers relates his sudden grasp of God's creative freedom as he observed his baby daughter. Noting the delicate convolutions of her "intricate, perfect ears" he had the stunning revelation that they were created neither by communism nor by random action of atoms in nature. He suddenly understood they could only be the result of God's purposeful design. He struggled mightily, for he also realized that such an insight presupposes God. It led to the profound truth that freedom has no meaning outside the context of God, its author.

Active faith, Christian or otherwise, demands much from devotees. Humans often appear to be no more than apathetic spiritual vagrants, whose beliefs and values are so diluted they don't have the resolve to hold any faith. The serpent doesn't care whether it is vigorous or lethargic. Any path will do, so long as it isn't the Way of the Lord. Jesus illustrates this in two parables, already noted, that will reappear throughout the book. The rich fool supposes he dominates his world by superior wit and strength, demonstrated by the earthly goods he amasses. At the other end of the spectrum is the servant with one talent, the epitome of slothfulness. He looks for any path to avoid physical, mental, or spiritual exertion. He expects his needs and desires to be fulfilled by others. Both believe that by denying God they can shape the world to fit their image, making them god by default. Satan is certain the die has been forever cast, since it is God Himself who declared the death sentence for disobedience. The way of the serpent deludes us into hoping this is freedom. It is, instead, complete slavery and the ultimate bondage. Chambers felt that losing this war leads to a woeful life of captivity, absent of freedom and creativity, dominated by the cruel control of humans over other humans.

The opposing resolve of "life, liberty and the pursuit of happiness" is explicitly addressed in the Declaration of Independence. It has been the energizing catalyst of America for all its history and today. It is the freedom to believe and worship as we choose, to speak our minds, to come and go, to assemble with any group, to defend ourselves, to own private property, to buy and sell, to earn a profit, to create individual wealth, and much more.

Bestowal of freedom is an omnipotent act. Statists would have us believe this is a prerogative of government. Do you see this is the same and ultimate either/or choice proffered in the garden? Make no mistake, there is a Creator. Either the human is god or God is, one or the other. Only God, the Creator, has the power to grant freedom. It is the essence of the Image of God.

The Bill of Rights is no dispenser of negative liberties, as argued by proponents of unrestrained government control. Instead, it limits the state's power over and against American citizens. The founding fathers did not consider it a collection of negative liberties. Rather, their view was the opposite. It is freedom's insurance policy and it was the precise guarantee they intended. The self-evident truths of these unalienable rights make us free, a free nation. It is America and the taproot of American Exceptionalism.

God did not abort. He restored the vital link to a fallen creation with generous, forgiving, and longsuffering behavior. As the man and woman made crude coverings to try and hide their guilt and shame, He sought out His beloved human beings, "Where are you?" Even as they stuttered, stammered, lied, and blamed each other, He responded as we never would. He furnished the antidote. It is His Son. A woman would give birth to this Son. Though wounded, He would offer the perfect and complete sacrifice. The devil would be defeated once and for all. God clothed the humans in animal skins and sent them out of the garden. His plan of salvation was underway. Anger did not deter God. Pride and ego did not cause Him to walk away. Love prevailed. It is classic entrepreneurial behavior, displaying prototypical risk-taking and initiative.

Amidst today's spiritual, social, political, and economic turmoil, we have received a unique and daring calling. Instead of submitting to the evil around us and within us, we are directed by God to "subdue...and have dominion" over creation. We are not called to be victims of Satan's whims or of the fallen world's circumstances. God's Kingdom, His rule and way of doing things, is to be alive in us as we are alive in the world. It is the way of the Lord.

Way of the Lord

Not long ago, a small church in an urban area struggled with isolation and decline. People from the neighborhood weren't attending. Membership was declining and growing older. Programs and planning seemed to yield no positive results. Worries about the death of the church filled the congregation. But one of the members, a quiet retired woman, was drawn to an old apartment complex next door to the church. She saw children and wanted them to know Jesus. On a warm South Texas spring day she sat at a table outside the apartment building, played Christian music, and dished out ice cream to children and parents. She engaged in conversations with the families and invited children to attend Vacation Bible School the following summer. Many accepted the invitation. She formed relationships, the first ever between the church and its neighbors. Her entrepreneurial behavior mirrored God's own.

This is the dominion God talks about in Genesis. This woman did what St. Paul emphasized to Galatian Christians as they struggled with legalism and corrupt ways of people around them. He said: *"The only thing that counts is faith expressing itself through love" (Galatians 5:6 NIV).*

As Christians, we understand we are not on this earth by chance or happenstance. As daughters and sons of the King, our lives are not created for a willy-nilly existence, but with a profound purpose – God's purpose. It is God's intention and will for us to be here. He has generously and graciously given us lives to be lived in the manner of faith and action He has demonstrated from the beginning. We don't have to do something earth-shaking. The way of the Lord is not about big programs, fame, expensive trappings, or large crowds. It is unconditional love, forgiveness, generosity, and individual action: *"Do not merely listen to the Word and so deceive yourselves. Do what it says." (James 1:22 NIV).*

Truth about the Way of the Lord is explained and illustrated throughout Scripture. The greatest demonstration is the life and death of Jesus, the last Adam. Jesus led by serving: *"...the Son of Man did not come to be served, but to serve, and to give his life as a ransom for many" (Matthew 20:28 NIV);* and: *"to seek and to save what was lost" (Luke 19:10 NIV).* Jesus stretched beyond the boundaries of selfish human convention. He set pride and fear aside, risking everything to reach *"the least of these" (Matthew 25:40 NIV).* He put His life on the line and gave it up to be the friend of sinners – our friend.

Too often we listen at His feet, watch Him in action, receive His gifts, and then fail to carry out His Will, often in spite of our best intentions. Church leaders of Jesus' day were paralyzed with self-centeredness and self-consciousness. They feared the risk of being out of line with the laws they had constructed around God's Word. They didn't want dirty hands from digging into the generous and gracious spirit of God's Word. Jesus condemned them:

"Woe to you, teachers of the law and Pharisees, you hypocrites! You shut the kingdom of heaven in men's faces. You

yourselves do not enter, nor will you let others who are trying to. Woe to you, teachers of the law and Pharisees, you hypocrites! You travel over land and sea to win a single convert, and when he becomes one, you make him twice as much a son of hell as you are" (Matthew 23:13–15 NIV).

His denunciation is on the mark. It is so easy to fall into a "me first" life and make ourselves god. This age-old trap leads us to believe we're number one. It leads to domination of ourselves over our fellowman.

Jesus takes a different path, setting the pace with unconditional love and mercy. He leaves His comfort zone and leads the way with self-sacrifice. Our lives are to be lived the same way. Don't take God's grace lightly. It demanded the death of His Son, who came to earth in human form to live a life of faith and action. Jesus, the last Adam, did not surrender to the way of the serpent, *"You will be like God" (Genesis 3:5 NIV).* He remained faithful and took the action that the first Adam was unable to carry out. But, there was an additional burden. As the last Adam, Jesus died as our substitute to satisfy God's justice. A blood ransom was paid on our behalf and now we do not have to suffer separation from God, unless we reject His free gift. Jesus took the risk and surrendered His life, trusting His Father to sustain and raise Him. God's unconditional love and generosity give us a new life, one that reflects the life of His Son.

"For just as through the disobedience of the one man the many were made sinners, so also through the obedience of the one man the many will be made righteous"(Romans 5:19 NIV); and "For as in Adam all die, so in Christ all will be made alive" (1 Corinthians 15:22 NIV).

Way of the Serpent

Albert Einstein is credited with the definition of insanity as doing the same thing over and over, expecting different results. There is no better manifestation of this than our unending quest to be god. Whittaker Chambers, in his intense personal struggle of faith, understood that the serpent's false promise, *"You will be like God"* is the "ultimate either/or" humans face every day. After surrendering to the serpent's temptation, the man and woman fashioned crude coverings for their bodies and tried to hide. They concocted a story and pointed the finger of blame at each other. Such denial, lies, and clinging to false reality typify humanity's brilliance. Our first inclination as fallen creatures is to collapse inwardly and grasp at straws. Apart from God, we function in selfishness and ignorance. The way of the serpent would have us travel that pathway to our eternal separation from God.

Human organizations are fallible. They forget intended missions. Bureaucracies, government and otherwise, let self-interest trump public service. Churches of this world decay and die because it becomes important to mollify certain individuals, rather than reach out to seek and save the lost. Families fracture because of disputes, indifference, and unwillingness to love and sacrifice for each other. Satan is not only anti-Christ, he is anti-people. He is anti-risk. He abhors the risk of unconditional love. He despises generosity. A recent TV commercial shows a person gazing at one technological gadget after another with a voice overlay, "I want it. I want it. I want it". It ends with the voice saying that "I" should buy them all for myself. Satan is delighted when "What's in it for me?" is our first, perhaps only, thought instead of choosing to serve God and fellowman. He is a liar and entices us to keep trying to make his original offer work, even though he knows it won't. If we can just do this or that better or differently this time we'll figure it out and be in control. Then we'll have the right system to reach our goal.

The dispute Elijah had with the prophets of Baal and Asherah offers an apt illustration. He and King Ahab agree to a contest to reveal the true God. Elijah challenged King Ahab:

"Now summon the people from all over Israel to meet me on Mount Carmel. And bring the four hundred and fifty prophets of Baal and the four hundred prophets of Asherah, who eat at Jezebel's table...Elijah went before the people and said, 'How long will you waver between two opinions? If the LORD is God, follow him; but if Baal is God, follow him" (1 Kings 18:19-21 NIV).

The ground rules were straightforward, so there could be no doubt. Each side would implore their respective God to consume a sacrifice with fire. The one who answered would be declared the true God.

The prophets of Baal and Asherah had the first chance. From morning till noon, they called on Baal and danced around the altar. Nothing happened. Then Elijah called the people together and reminded Israel that they were God's chosen people. Wood was placed on the altar, and a trench was dug around it. Then water was poured on the altar, the wood, and into the trench around the sacrificial structure. This was repeated three times.

"...Elijah stepped forward and prayed: "O LORD, God of Abraham, Isaac, and Israel, let it be known today that you are God in Israel, and that I am your servant and have done all these things at your command. Answer me, O LORD, answer me, so these people will know that you, O LORD, are God, and that you are turning their hearts back again...Then the fire of the LORD fell

27

and burned up the sacrifice, the wood, the stones and the soil, and also licked up the water that was in the trench. When all the people saw this, they fell prostrate and cried, 'The LORD, he is God - the LORD, he is God'" (1 Kings 18:36–39 NIV).

The false prophets embody the human futility of striving to be god. It is foolishness and leads only to destruction, but we seem incapable of giving it up. What is so irresistible? With blind ego, we adopt and repeat one iteration after another, trying to take God's place. We construct systems, traditions, organizations, and rules. We inflate our abilities and pack schedules with busywork. We plunge into personal striving and push people away who might "interrupt" the real business of what we decide our self-god wants us to do. We ignore truth and seek to create the serpent's would-be truth, hoping it will make us feel better, more important, and more in control.

From his first lie, the devil's deceitful personality is exposed. He is full of half-truths and skilled at sounding like God, appearing to be virtuous, and seeming to make sense. *"...Satan himself masquerades as an angel of light" (2 Corinthians 11:14 NIV).* Being "like God" is a clever but misleading alteration of being made in God's image and likeness. It is a statement of equality, of being the same. It is a competitive assertion of challenge and opposition.

Image of God

The truth of being made in God's "image" is in stark contrast to being "like God". Scripture says: *"So God created man in His own image, in the image of God He created him; male and female He created them" (Genesis 1:27 NIV).*

This is a declaration of love, an expression of giving. Humans were created as the "apple of God's eye." God created them to be in relationship with Him, to be His partners and friends. God's deep and abiding love for humanity elevated people. We are the crown jewel of creation. That unfathomable love is seen fully in the sacrifice of Jesus for the redemption of humanity. Listen to Jesus, our brother:

"Both the one who makes men holy and those who are made holy are of the same family. So Jesus is not ashamed to call them brothers" (Hebrews 2:11 NIV).

As His partners, God assigned mankind a momentous task:

"Be fruitful and increase in number; fill the earth and subdue it. Rule over the fish of the sea and over the birds of the heavens and over every living creature that moves on the ground" (Genesis 1:28 NIV).

This isn't gibberish from a bored Creator playing with a new "human" toy. He is serious about this exclusive domain and intends real and earnest work to be shared with humans whom He has named children and heirs. His actions sanctify the work in which each of us is to be engaged. Not one of His other creatures is capable of such a partnership. Only humans have received the same creative capacity as the Creator. The Hebrew "radah" is used in the Scripture reference above. It means "to rule". It denotes significant responsibility and evokes our calling: *"...we are God's fellow workers" (I Corinthians 3:9 NIV).*

How are we to accomplish this? If we surrender to the serpent's temptations and lies, it is truly daunting and overwhelming. But, we are not tossed into the world to fend for ourselves. Through our substitute, Jesus, God's presence and power are accessible to us all. Creation is filled with His resources, visible and invisible, for our use and His glory. More significantly, we are given a creative and rational mind along with an intentional attitude to carry out our calling. This is a major component of God's image. It is deep and unfathomable, a part of His very essence. It is the spirit that overflows into and through us back to God and to our fellowman. It honors us as His coworkers:

"For the LORD gives wisdom, and from his mouth come knowledge and understanding" (Proverbs 2:6 NIV); and:

"...wisdom will enter your heart, and knowledge will be pleasant to your soul. Discretion will protect you, and understanding will guard you." (Proverbs 2:10-11 NIV).

This gift of creativity and rational sensibility did not cease to function when humans submitted and committed themselves to the serpent's false truth. In business and commerce, for example, humans "create" products and wealth by using their minds to re-formulate matter found in the earth and universe. Seeping crude oil was not only transformed by 19th and 20th Century minds into hundreds of valuable petro-chemical products, but the minds of native Americans created useful products as far back as the early 15th Century. Sand is almost 100% silica and virtually worthless until it is reformulated by human creativity and initiative into silicon microchips and innumerable technology products. More astonishingly, humans use their minds to translate intangible ideas into structures such as the Periodic Table of Elements, mathematical formulae, and processes used to produce a wide variety of services and goods. We enjoy music, painting, dance, and literature. All are from the human mind, God's gift of Himself.

What a precious possession. The human mind constitutes the most significant and perhaps total variance between humans and the rest of creation. We are the only creatures with the capacity to reason, deal with abstract concepts, strategize, devise languages, and much more. When the Creator directs mankind to subdue and have dominion over His creation, a creative attitude is assumed, one that is eager to steward God's gifts and resources. Faith that expresses itself in love continually recreates the world in God's image. New developments glorify God. Serving others becomes service to Christ Himself. Lives become changed and brand new not only for now, but forever. This makes it possible to understand what Jesus meant when He said:

"I tell you the truth, anyone who has faith in me will do what I have been doing. He will do even greater things than these..." *(John 14:12 NIV).*

God's grace and love entrusts us with His own power.

Our active involvement in the way of the Lord accomplishes much more than merely building a strong economy and creating wealth. By entering God's calling we accomplish the requirements of His greatest command:

"Love the Lord your God with all your heart and with all your soul and with all your mind" and *"Love your neighbor as yourself"* *(Matthew 22:37–40 NIV).*

This is self-sacrificing love without ego. It is on display when we combine matter God created with the gifts of His knowledge, understanding, and wisdom to create everything needed to serve God and fellowman. This first principle of love is acted on when we use the mind to conceive and develop ideas, processes, solutions, art, music, and all things that edify and bring wholeness to others. The use of technology has the potential to serve and bless untold numbers. God sets the pace, first sending His Son and then us, creative and motivated people to share His gifts.

Entrepreneur is a term normally limited to business. It is often characterized as extraordinary and mysterious as well as a bit intimidating. Some are awestruck at the wealth created by people like Warren Buffett, Bill Gates, and Sam Walton. In fact, creation of wealth, the first borne of labors, is not mysterious at all. Neither is it sinful, unless its motive and use are under the destructive way of the serpent. David recognized this. As resources were gathered to build the temple, he prayed and praised God as the source:

"Wealth and honor come from you; you are the ruler of all things. In your hands are strength and power to exalt and give strength to all" (1 Chronicles 29:12 NIV).

God bestows extraordinary gifts and talents. We are called to steward them in the way of the Lord, the way of love. Our mission is to be creative, generous, audacious, and self-sacrificial.

Hesitating or using God's resources in a limited manner constitutes incomplete stewardship. It is wasteful. It dishonors the Giver. It is selfish. It is the servant with one talent burying it in the ground rather than using it to bless God and humanity. Such action reveals its true nature. It is nothing more than an attempt to be our own god. It is the way of the serpent. On the other hand, if we believe God and have faith as small as a "mustard seed," we are able to tell a mountain: *"'Move from here to there' and it will move. Nothing will be impossible for you"* (Matthew 17:20 NIV).

Sadly, we often revert to the upside down way of the serpent and ignore the breadth and depth of the Creator's resources available for our use. So, we retreat and exclude extravagant options. We play it "safe" and limit God to our puny and incomplete plans, the plans of would-be gods.

God calls us to something greater and more meaningful. We can't grasp this until we are turned, once again, right side up. He gives us gifts of faith and action. With God, nothing is impossible. He gives us His creative Spirit that always takes the risk of love.

Entrepreneurial DNA

God's call to Abram was direct: *"Leave your country, your people and your father's household and go to the land I will show you"* (Genesis 12:1 NIV).

Abram didn't know the destination or the route. Yet, he took the prescribed risk and action. He trusted God's Word. In a later exchange he lamented that he had no heir, thinking his business manager, Eliezer of Damascus, would inherit his estate. God responded with a bold promise:

"'This man will not be your heir, but a son coming from your own body will be your heir.' He took him outside and said, 'Look up at the heavens and count the stars - if indeed you can count them.'

Then he said to him, 'So shall your offspring be'" (Genesis 15:4–5 NIV).

Abram believed what God told him. It was credited to him as righteousness. Abram trusted God's promise and took the risk. In his faith and action he demonstrated the very entrepreneurism of the model entrepreneur.

God intends no less for us. His call is just as direct. Are you a person of faith and action? Are you a hearer AND doer of God's Word? Are you heeding Jesus' call to follow? Do you remember that God created you, re-claimed you, and called you?

"You are the salt of the earth...the light of the world. A city on a hill cannot be hidden...let your light shine before men, that they may see your good deeds and praise your Father in heaven" (Matthew 5:13-16 NIV).

Are you waiting for a time when there is no risk?

Perhaps you are thinking, "I'm not the adventurous type. I'm not an enterprising person. I can't venture into unknown territory and take momentous actions like those of Christopher Columbus or Abraham Lincoln. I could never improve the lives of average people like Thomas Edison or George Washington Carver. I'm no Martin Luther or Martin Luther King, correcting the flow of societal thinking and ready to take a stand for a new way of life." Look at the child who takes a parent's hand and then proceeds unworried across a busy street. Or, consider my gardener who trusts his ability to do the job and earn sufficient income to support his family. He follows that trust by working however hard and long he must to accomplish his goals. Both are entrepreneurs as much as any famous or not-so-famous individual who is or is not known as such. American history overflows with millions of individuals from every corner of the globe who arrived with only the tattered clothes on their backs, but who also had faith in their convictions and undying determination to persevere when others might give up.

What is this intangible force that has become such a hallmark of the United States? Might this "entrepreneurial DNA" be rooted in the heart of God? Could the quest for freedom in our nation, the risk-it-all attitude of those who ventured to this country, be bound up in the very nature of God? Is it possible to discover a creative and energetic Spirit that will enliven us as God's own children – and heirs? Can we trace connections of entrepreneurial actions back to a God who has even greater plans for us and has commissioned us to use His gifts in and for the world into which He has placed us?

If you dare to live in the lavish love of God, you will find answers. You will follow boldly in the steps of the entrepreneurial God, His entrepreneurial Son, and the entrepreneurial Spirit. How is God breathing His exciting breath of life into you? How is He calling you to a faith adventure in a new place right where you are? How is He shaping you right now for His extraordinary and entrepreneurial purposes? Read on and rediscover the life He offers you. This is your life, not the life of someone else. So, live it!

Chapter 1

Discussion Questions

1. What is true freedom and what are some obstacles to freedom?

2. Talk about the contrast between "the way of the Lord" and "the way of the serpent."

3. How does God's grace fit into the life of faith and action?

4. Discuss the notion that "entrepreneurial DNA" is rooted in the heart of God.

5. Think about and discuss the final questions of this chapter:
   - How is God breathing His exciting breath of life into you?

   - How is He calling you to a faith adventure in a new place right where you are?

   - How is He shaping you right now for His extraordinary and entrepreneurial purposes?

Chapter Two

Entrepreneurial Model

Entrepreneurial Behavior

America's free enterprise system has been an economic juggernaut and the envy of the rest of the world. Americans "DID build that" and even though it has been in a slight stall, momentum can be recaptured by going back to basics.

This economic success is no mystery. It commenced with early colonists and actually was part of the catalyst that brought about the American Revolution. Free enterprise was introduced and has been nurtured, expanded, and sustained in no small part because of individuals and small groups who participate as buyers and sellers in the marketplace. They invest personal resources, tangible and intangible, and apply discipline with determination. The behavior they display fits "hand in glove" with the definition of entrepreneur found at www.dictionary.com, "a person who organizes and manages any enterprise, especially a business, usually with considerable risk and initiative." Two character traits emerge:

1. Risk (risk-taking) is "the potential that a chosen action or activity will lead to a loss." Risk-takers have unwavering faith and trust in their talents, capabilities, and expert knowledge, which is often instinctive.

2. Independent initiative may be described as an indefatigable motivation and drive to succeed. Initiative-takers don't expect or desire help from others. Self-reliance, determination, and tireless discipline are the driving forces (http://www.dictionary.com).

Non-Business Environment

Most analysis and discussion of entrepreneurial conduct is focused on individuals engaged in commercial enterprises. Yet, even casual examination reveals abundant evidence of similar behavior outside the realm of business profits and losses. The definition cited above recognizes this with the inclusive phrase, "any enterprise." The characteristics of risk-taking and individual initiative are displayed by people in all walks of life and life situations. They are obvious in the work of an accomplished artist, the execution of playing skills by an athlete, or in a parent who builds and maintains rapport through a maze of challenges that must be overcome in raising children. They form an endless line: astronauts, first responders, homemakers, doctors, teachers, store clerks, cab drivers, combat commanders, clergy, and volunteers. Across the spectrum of life, countless people are constantly engaged in this behavior.

God & Creation

While the term entrepreneur arose in 19th Century France, the concept is very much older. The Genesis creation story plainly lays out its fundamentals. It gives a glimpse of the power and energy available to us not just in business, but in all facets of life. A fuller application of its principles enables us to not only revitalize America's economy, but to better fulfill God's directive to subdue and have dominion over His creation.

The Genesis creation account tells us that God said, *"...Let us make man in our image..." (Genesis 1:26 NIV)* To this point, God had said, *"Let there be"* and light, darkness, time, the universe (all universes), earth, all forms of life, environment, and seasons come into being without specific action directed at a particular object or creature. Why the special attention to His final creation? God bestows His very image on this last and special creature. The omnipotent, omniscient, omnipresent Master of all dares to give the crown of His creation the freedom to walk with Him or to reject Him. In this action, the Creator models risk and faith, the first characteristic of entrepreneurial behavior. Why would God take such a risk? The inescapable conclusion is that He wanted an interpersonal relationship based on faith and trust. If not, the Creator could have simply created humanity the same way He had brought about the rest of the animal kingdom and the rest of creation: *"...Let there be..."*

Like a bad dream, the man and woman allowed themselves to be lured by the false promise of the serpent, *"You will be like God" (Genesis 3:5 NIV)*. Never forget that Satan, above all else, is a liar. He is the prince of lies. So, how did God respond? Why didn't He destroy the wretched creatures? Wait! Look again at His purpose. God desired a relationship with the humans He had created, so He stayed "on task" and took the initiative. This is the second trait of entrepreneurial behavior. God sent His Son, not to administer justice and judgment. His mission was to return us to the relationship God originally sought. This is still His desire. Jesus did what the first Adam didn't do. He remained true to the Word of the Master. Through the life and death of this "last Adam" God enables us, by simple faith, to reconnect with Him in the relationship He intended from eternity. It means we can be put back on the path to our intended and eternal home, to be in a relationship with the Creator forever. This is the "Divine Model" and an astonishing display that reveals a loving God as the Master Entrepreneur.

Last Adam

Jesus, our substitute, is described by theologians as the "second" or "last" Adam". St. Paul explains to the church in Corinth:

"'The first man Adam became a living being'; the last Adam, a life-giving spirit. The spiritual did not come first, but the natural, and after that the spiritual. The first man was of the dust of the earth, the second man from heaven. As was the earthly man, so are those who are of the earth; and as is the man from heaven, so also are those who are of heaven. And just as we have borne the likeness of the earthly man, so shall we bear the likeness of the man from heaven" (I Corinthians 15:45-49 NIV).

Jesus did not take human form to merely show us what God is like. God reveals Himself impressively, if we're paying attention. Jesus came to demonstrate, by His life, God's expectation of mankind. More importantly, He came as a ransom so we can receive a restored relationship with the Creator God and not have to pay the price of eternal separation. As part of His Father's call, Jesus lived the life God intends of humans. It is the life the first Adam (humans) was supposed to live, but did not. Jesus lived it in the "image of God," the same that Adam and Eve lived prior to their ill-fated decision to declare themselves to be their own gods. To err is NOT human. Jesus is the "true" human. To err is the way of the serpent. During Jesus' "humanity" on earth, He chose the way of the Lord over the way of the serpent. The temptations were real. He *"...was tempted in every way, just as we are-yet was without sin"* (Hebrews 4:15 NIV). He lived a perfect life, one which we are told to emulate: *"Be perfect, therefore, as your heavenly Father is perfect" (Matthew 5:48 NIV).* Over fifty times in Scripture we are told to be perfect or given examples of those God has declared perfect because of faith. This mandate reveals our sin for what it truly is as well as our utter helplessness. In one of Jesus' parables, the debt of the unmerciful servant was insurmountable. His only recourse was to throw himself at the mercy of the Master. The Master didn't forgive the debt because of any worthiness he spotted in this ingrate. Guilty, as charged. It was pure grace. So it is with us. When the mirror of God shines on us, we stand naked before His judgment. Which part of our need for a Savior don't we understand?

God's Resources

Chris Ortiz makes a compelling case at his website (www.reigninlife.com) where he describes the Creator God as "the ultimate craftsman...the model for entrepreneurial calling." He poses two questions: "(1) How did God create His enterprise? ... (2) What was His work ethic"? The parallel between the two character traits we are examining and his two questions is self-apparent. His answers are eye-opening and provide fresh insights (www.reigninlife.com).

As to the first, he cites:

"By faith we understand that the universe was formed at God's command, so that what is seen was not made out of what was visible" (Hebrews 11:3 NIV).

Some interpret this to mean God created things out of nothing (no thing). Ortiz notes that something not visible is not "no thing". He reasons that the end of the verse, *"...not made out of what was visible"*, means God created everything using His invisible resources, of which three are identified: knowledge, wisdom, and understanding. Ortiz gives several proof texts.

1. *"By wisdom the Lord laid the earth's foundations, by understanding He set the heavens in place; by His knowledge the deeps were divided, and the clouds let drop the dew" (Proverbs 3:19-20 NIV).*

2. *"But God made the earth by his power; He founded the world by His wisdom and stretched out the Heavens by His understanding" (Jeremiah 10:12 NIV).*

3. *"In the beginning was the Word, and the Word was with God, and the Word was God. The same was in the beginning with God. All things were made by Him; and without Him was not any thing made that was made" (John 1:1-3 NIV).*

4. *"For this cause we also, since the day we heard it, do not cease to pray for you, and to desire that you might be filled with the Knowledge of His will in all wisdom and spiritual understanding" (Colossians 1:9 NIV).*

Although God's resources are invisible, they are very real and present in His creation. They are certainly not "no thing." The upshot is that God's resources are still here and His intent is for us to discover and use them, following God's command to "...subdue and have dominion..." over what He created. We're talking about the human mind and its capacity for rational and creative thought. God's words are not difficult to understand:

"...for it is God who works in you to will and to act according to His good purpose" (Philippians 2:13 NIV).

He commissions us to discover and use the resources He gave as part of His image, particularly knowledge, understanding and wisdom. These and other resources are articulated more fully in Chapter 8, The Image of God. With these we are to continuously re-create the world in God's image.

It is clear in the parable of talents that this is what the servants with five and two talents did. It is equally evident this is what the servant with one talent did NOT do. The failure of the third servant didn't occur because he had only one talent. He would have failed no matter how many talents he possessed, because he was totally absent of intent and attitude. God wants us to use knowledge, understanding, and wisdom to the fullest, regardless of the talents we have received from Him.

As to the second question, regarding God's work ethic, Ortiz hypothesizes that in creation itself we find the basic structure of our life calendars:

"...so on the seventh day He rested from all His work." (Genesis 2:2 NIV); and: *"Six days you shall labor and do all your work, but the seventh day is a Sabbath to the Lord your God..." (Exodus 20:9-10 NIV)*.

God made His whole enterprise in a six-day workweek, using His knowledge, understanding, and wisdom, and He wants us to pattern our lives after Him. Creation is filled with His knowledge, understanding, and wisdom, which we are to seek and use.

We learn to do this through education (not just school, especially in today's Internet world) and experience. It is revealed to the greatest measure when we immerse ourselves in God's

Word. In the section of Matthew identified as "The Sermon on the Mount" Jesus addresses the issue of being "perfect". He says: *"Be perfect, therefore, as your heavenly Father is perfect" (Matthew 48:5 NIV)*.

Jesus accomplished this with God's resources of knowledge, understanding, and wisdom to stay connected with God for guidance in His earthly life. Likewise, we are to stay connected with the source of our power. It is a key part of the relationship we again enjoy with God through Jesus. God's *knowledge, understanding, and wisdom* saturate His world. They are the source for all mankind has ever created or done. This includes spiritual matters, for these same three elements are the resources for understanding God's Word and His Will in our lives. It is impossible to separate secular life from spiritual life. The secular parts of our lives are to be lived in faith. They are intertwined.

Ortiz's final point is that nonbelievers do not recognize God's invisible resources as such or acknowledge Him as the giver. Mankind supposes its knowledge, understanding, and wisdom are somehow of its own making. It is as if the laws of gravity, physics, and nature do not exist unless a human discovers them. Mankind proudly displays the creation of airplanes, computers, and cellphones as though the technology itself were of its own making, rather than recognizing the creativity and initiative as well as the raw materials are extracted from God's world, bestowed at creation. The vestige of God's image, twisted and warped by the way of the serpent, is used to misconstrue and parade the achievements of mankind as its own. In fact, God is the source.

We receive His knowledge, understanding, and wisdom along with His complete creation so that we may exercise dominion over the earth, as He intends.

Expanded Meaning of Entrepreneur

While the definition of entrepreneur remains largely intact, as provided by www.dictionary.com, a broader application than business and commerce emerges. In particular, those who understand God to be their Creator and Savior, can argue a "prior" claim to these characteristics:

1. Risk* (risk-taking). Christian faith, by which a person's ultimate destiny is taken out of personal control, is the ultimate risk. *"Now faith is being sure of what we hope for and certain of what we do not see" (Hebrews 11:1 NIV).*
2. Individual initiative. While salvation, through Christ, is intended for everyone, faith is an entirely personal matter, between God and the individual, without reliance on any human person (including oneself) or agency. *"...continue to work out your salvation with fear and trembling, for it is God who works in you to will and to act according to His good purpose" (Philippians 2:12-13 NIV).*

*For the purpose of better understanding throughout the book, risk, faith, and trust are used interchangeably to describe the first character trait of entrepreneurial behavior.

Chapter 2

Discussion Questions

1. How is entrepreneurial conduct a possibility in your life today?

2. How does Jesus' work as the "last Adam" encourage and motivate you?

3. Discuss the unique attributes and distinctive definitions of knowledge, understanding, and wisdom.

4. What does it mean that risk is when "a person's ultimate destiny is taken out of personal control"?

5. How is individual initiative related to a life of faith?

Chapter Three

American Entrepreneurism

Entrepreneurial Behavior

At the outset, this book was intended to inspire and encourage individuals at the grassroots level to be positive forces in an American economic recovery. Record unemployment and negative economic news seemed to be the daily fare. Yet, Americans are people of action and not easily discouraged or intimidated. Challenges are a welcome invitation to engage and overcome. It is worthwhile to help people uncover and use their entrepreneurial talents toward this end. While the focus of the book has shifted, its original idea is still an objective. Thus, the content in the next three chapters deals largely with free enterprise. This is not meant to be even a beginning business or economics course. It is, for the most part, background information.

Business Risk

Certainly, there is more to a successful business than trust in one's ability to overcome all obstacles and independent initiative. A profitable company employs staff with a broad set of skills in such areas as finance, accounting, production, marketing and sales, distribution, management, human resources, and customer service. There is, however, a substantive and substantial difference between entrepreneurial traits and business skills. The former are inborn and non-cognitive, while the latter are rational. Business skills can be taught to individuals with average or better intelligence. Courses that impart such skills are the mainstay of business school curricula. Risk-taking and individual initiative, on the other hand, emanate from the emotional and attitudinal part of a person's makeup. This is not to say that it can only occur spontaneously or unpredictably. Part of the book's purpose, in fact, is to help people uncover and utilize these qualities in an organized fashion.

Many have a perception that entrepreneurs are a rare and exceptional class, at times eccentric and usually genius. Often, there is also an assumption that their only drive is to make as much money as possible. Stereotypes abound. Businesses that start with full-scale operations are quite rare. They usually begin small, often with one person. Stories of starting a company in a garage or an abandoned building are often true. After an often-difficult and uneven beginning, a start-up might grow to be well-known: Thomas Edison (GE), Henry Ford (Ford), Steven Jobs (Apple), Mary Kay Ash (Mary Kay), Samuel Johnson (S.C. Johnson), Ray Kroc (McDonalds), Carl and Barbara Paul (Golfsmith), Truett Cathy (Chick-fil-A), and John Schnatter (Papa John's Pizza).

Looking only at successful enterprises, however, misses the critical effect and constant threat of risk. First, a start-up operation has no safety net and the odds that it will survive are perilous at best. In his research on new business survival rates, Dr. Scott Shane, Professor of Entrepreneurial Studies at Case Western University, has found that many more new businesses fail than succeed (http://smallbiztrends.com/2012/05/businesses-face-high-rates-of-mortality.html).

Second, risk is ever-present. Do you recognize these former "household" names: A&P, Bell & Howell, American

Motors, Arthur Andersen, NCR, EBASCO, Fairchild Semiconductor, U.S. Steel, Montgomery Ward, or Oldsmobile? All were once successful, making investors and stockholders wealthy. Today some are smaller; many have merged with other companies, but most no longer exist. One day you're thriving and the next you are fighting for survival.

Third, all company operations have financial results. If revenues are higher than expenses, the net result is a profit. If expenses are more than revenues, the net result is a loss. Owners and investors are pleased when they receive financial returns from profitable ventures. For example, Walmart made a fortune for founder Samuel Walton. Though he died in 1992, his heirs annually rank among the wealthiest Americans. The negative side of the ledger is not so pleasant. Losses don't evaporate into a business netherworld. They are not absorbed by federal or other agencies. Real dollars are lost by flesh and blood people and embody the very definition of risk.

Why do people take the personal risk of a business venture? As a rule, start-up companies require substantial funding and considerable time to become successful. Business risk does not refer to foolish gambles like buying a lottery ticket or blindly stepping into a busy street. It has to do with faith and trust an individual has in his or her talents, capabilities, and expert knowledge of products and markets. Free enterprise rewards successful inventors and investors, often substantially. This is the reason such funding is called "venture" capital. The net result is the creation of billions of dollars in new wealth every year.

Justice & Morality

Economics has been famously defined by English economist Lionel Robins as "…the science which studies human behavior as a relationship between given ends and scarce means which have alternate uses." It is of considerable importance to note that Economics is a behavioral science, as opposed to a natural or hard science like chemistry or physics. Pure science is predictable. Human behavior is not (Robins, Lionel. <u>An essay on the Nature and Significance of Economic Science</u>, p. 16)

Modern economic systems operate either on the basis of free and open markets or according to the dictates imposed by centralized planning and controls. The former follows the principles of capitalism and is represented by America's free enterprise system. It is based on the theoretical writings of Adam Smith, Friedrich von Hayek, Milton Friedman and others. At the other end of the scale is a centrally planned and controlled economic system. Its most extreme example is the collectivist economic system of Soviet Russia that ultimately collapsed. While today's versions of centrally-planned economies are milder, there should be no mistake that their origins are based on theoretical constructs of Karl Marx. John Maynard Keynes is its contemporary and most recognized proponent. Neither system is found in its unsullied form, each with elements of its counterpart. Philosophically, however, one or the other is the main source of a system's core values and guiding principles.

Although free enterprise has served America well, there is debate over which economic system is best for America. Free enterprise proponents espouse individual freedom and initiative, with classic entrepreneurial traits as its driving forces. Detractors argue that free enterprise is inspired by greed and denies the fundamental rights of people, but have no explanation why hundreds of thousands eagerly cascade over the borders into a supposedly racist country where ruthless and evil capitalism takes unfair advantage of an impoverished and persecuted subclass. Conversely, backers of a centrally planned economy contend it is driven by equality and fairness. Opponents point out that equality and fairness, as well as greed, are human attributes and qualities that are present in any economic system. Advocates of free enterprise consider centralized control an impediment to economic growth, because it removes incentives to work and promotes reliance on entitlements. It penalizes success and confiscates incomes of those in the work force.

The debate turns on the issues of justice and morality. According to the <u>Concise Oxford English Dictionary</u>, "just" is defined as "morally right or fair." Both are concerned with principles of right and wrong or conforming to standards of behavior and character based on those principles. Additional descriptors include "ethical, honest, upright, fair, and principled." These terms are all associated with specific behaviors. While a social structure such as capitalism or collectivism may or may not recognize and observe just and moral principles, neither can be just and moral (or unjust and immoral) in and of itself. It is only people who can bestow or carry out just and moral actions toward other people. So which economic system, the free market or a planned economy, better facilitates ethical, honest, upright, fair, and principled behavior of people toward others? Which is more just and moral?

Before addressing economic justice and morality, however, there is a "log in the eye" matter that should be clarified. Comparisons of free enterprise and a centrally planned economy often make an erroneous assumption that the economic outcomes of the two systems are the same. Nothing could be further from the truth. In a planned economy, critical business decisions are controlled by appointed planning groups, as opposed to the private sector. Supply and demand are fixed, as are wages. A socialist economy provides no incentive for innovation or improvement of product quality, because competition among private companies is disrupted and distorted by interference from bureaucrats who often are quite ignorant of the issues being addressed. Free enterprise may require regulatory controls, but historically it is the only option for consistent economic growth.

Centrally Planned Economic System

In a centrally planned economy, virtually all economic decisions are made by a government agency. Unlike free enterprise in which decisions are made by private citizens and business owners, a centrally planned economy seeks to control basic economic variables such as the allocation of resources, what goods are produced, and at what price. In addition, the government decides what job an individual will be assigned, the number of work hours, and wages. It is assumed that the market does not work in the best interests of people. Proponents believe that in order to assure that social and national objectives are met, it is imperative for economic decisions to be made by a central agency. Note the not-so-subtle shift from what is good for people to what is good for society. This is not a safe assumption.

It is eye-opening to look at the position of Marx vis-à-vis profits, against which he raged. Yet, he ignored the issue of losses. His central assertion on the subject was that the bourgeoisie, i.e., the middle class, collectively owns the means of production, manipulates the economic system by pre-setting profits, and then forces other components to conform.

The mechanisms and functions of an economic system cannot be pre-set or manipulated by a central planning group or any other authority. More than difficult, it is impossible. We are still paying the price from the time when control of America's economy was usurped in response to the Great Depression. It was not Keynesian economics that led America out of that morass. The country was shocked out of it by World War II. A "great awakening" emerged at the war's end. Americans discovered they are exceptionally adept at free enterprise. Introduction of the G.I. Bill added education to the recent "cross-cultural" experiences of millions of war veterans. American Exceptionalism became a reality in which everyone could participate. Free enterprise isn't a pure science. It cannot be controlled any more than the stock market. Manipulation of the elements of free enterprise most often leads to economic catastrophe. Thomas Sowell offers a brilliant essay on the topic in the first section of Basic Economics: A Citizen's Guide to the Economy. It should be required reading (Sowell, Thomas. Basic Economics: a Citizen's Guide to the Economy).

For some, the term capitalism is what the late linguistic icon, S.I. Hayakawa, labeled a "flag" word, projecting such strong emotional content that its meaning is obscured. If economic debate is framed in the preconceived context of a human failing such as greed, the issue will never be resolved. Free enterprise does not succeed because of greed. It is quite the opposite. It succeeds because it necessitates individuals to disregard personal preferences and focus on needs and desires of others. When Einstein said, "Keep things as simple as possible, but no simpler", he could have been talking about the description of a successful business: "Find a need and fill it." The need to be filled is that of consumers, not sellers (Hayakawa, S.I., <u>Language in Thought and Action</u>. Words with built-in judgments. 1939. Ch. 5-8).

A socialist economic system is managed and controlled by would-be elite members of society, who view themselves as capable of fulfilling this complex role. The premise is flawed. It is not feasible for an appointed central planning group to successfully maneuver an economic system. Decisions by such groups are based on inaccurate, incomplete, and untimely information, fraught with the danger of unintended and negative consequences as well as graft and fraud.

Under socialist economic systems, the recipients of government largess are short-changed. They become special-interest voting blocs, pawns that insure a continuation of graft and fraud. Who's checking the checkers? This is not a display of justice or morality, but a manifestation of tyranny. A centrally controlled and managed economy is ill-fated. Results are anemic and disappointing at best. At worst, the result is likely to be dysfunctional and disastrous. The outcomes are usually deeper debt and ever-expanding controls.

Since the initial introduction of socialist economics in the U.S., it has been promoted as the best system for the government to take care of its citizens. Yet, it is staffed with career politicians, bureaucrats, and lawyers who pursue primarily their own interests. The pensions created by bureaucrats for government retirees exponentially drive up government costs. The bank bailouts in the first decade of the millennium have been a collective disaster. Bankers should be bankers, not hedge fund managers who trade with other people's money and keep profits while passing losses back to the government. Politicians all too often promote solutions that only consolidate more power to themselves in an all-too bipartisan manner.

The principal safeguards of free enterprise are simple, efficient, and effective. An enterprise that doesn't keep costs and quality in line with competition disappears into bankruptcy and private investors must absorb the financial losses. Outside a typical management "chain of command", there are no checks and balances in a centrally-controlled economy.

Free Enterprise Economic System

Free enterprise is rooted in America's earliest days. Seeking to create a nation and culture rooted in freedom and justice, colonists sensed inequities in the taxation and other controls imposed by England. Moral, intellectual, political, commercial, and other disputes led to the Revolutionary War. In the infant nation, the free market faced minimal government interference. Significantly, the same year the Declaration of Independence was signed, citizens of the young nation, looking for a just and moral system, were inspired by Scotsman Adam Smith. His book, The Wealth of Nations, energized Americans with its message that an individual can achieve success and prosperity with a mindset of self-reliance, honesty, determination, and hard work.

The free market principles he championed continue to inspire and motivate Americans to thrive through personal creativity and resolute determination. Even before the War of 1812, this spirit of growth and expansion manifested itself when President Jefferson engineered the Louisiana Purchase in 1803, and the next year instigated its exploration by funding the Lewis and Clark Expedition.

American free enterprise draws on two Constitutional values. The first is liberty. A free market functions best in a society that recognizes the inherent freedom and independence of people. As noted earlier, these include freedoms to assemble and speak freely, to follow the dictates of one's conscience, to come and go as one pleases, to possess private property, to choose what one will own or buy or sell, to pursue whatever job and career one desires, to possess and retain financial earnings, and much more. The source of freedom is a key point, addressed specifically in the Declaration of Independence: "We hold these truths to be self-evident, that all men are created equal, that they are endowed by their Creator with certain unalienable Rights, that among these are Life, Liberty, and the pursuit of Happiness."

Just and moral behavior cannot be taken for granted. Economic growth is often explosive and appropriate regulations are required to curb excessive and abusive practices. At times, actions of unscrupulous business people not only violate the values espoused by free enterprise, but breach the very principles of the Constitution. The founders understood this and provided protections through what is called the "Rule of Law." Like all checks and balances, it has to be neutral and impartial. It is critical that everyone, without exception and without regard to position or status, be treated equally under the law. Clearly, "too big to fail," was not a good economic or ethical practice in the 18th Century. It is equally harmful today. The legislative branch is authorized to regulate business practices with measures like anti-monopoly and antitrust legislation and the national income tax that was enacted in 1913. Congress is also active in the negotiation of trade and tax treaties with other countries.

Freedom exacts a price. More than 1.25 million Americans have died protecting the liberty of their fellow Americans. This vigilance must focus inside as well as outside, for a government strong enough to protect its citizens by its might is also capable of using that same power to impose itself in areas it should not. As powerful as America's government may be, it does not possess the omnipotence, omniscience, or omnipresence of divine providence to grant or deny liberty. Human minds and organizations are incapable of monitoring the non-physical realms of thought, loyalty, motivation, and attitude. Freedom is not subject to the decision of an appointed committee, the vote of Congress, or an executive order from the President. America's founding fathers understood that only our Creator is capable of granting freedom.

The second constitutional value is equal treatment. "Rule of law" is a cornerstone of democracy. Equality is unambiguously addressed by the founders. "All men are created equal," represents their intent to assure all citizens equal opportunity and uniform treatment. Equality of outcome is not the intent or goal. Equality is not administered by taking money from those who have earned it and giving it to those who didn't. Never mind that more than a healthy portion is kept by those who take it upon themselves to re-distribute it. Fairness is not served by amassing massive debt for food stamps, health care, retirement, and other entitlements, leaving it to future generations to pay the bills. The purposely-misleading argument that entitlements somehow "level the playing field" is usually a justification for confiscating money that belongs to others. Justice is not served by showing favoritism to a group of companies because they are "too big to fail." Some confuse being pro-free market with being pro-business. Crony-capitalism isn't free enterprise. It is only corny-ism that reflects central-control advocates. It is a serious breach of public trust.

In the frame of mind that focuses on liberty, it is not difficult to understand why free enterprise is America's economic system of choice. It meshes seamlessly with democratic tenets. It is the very personification of the justice, morals, principles, and values our forefathers laid out in America's founding documents: The Declaration of Independence, the U.S. Constitution, and Bill of Rights. The Declaration of Independence points like a laser: "We hold these truths to be self-evident, that all men are created equal, that they are endowed by their Creator with certain inalienable Rights, that among these are Life, Liberty and the pursuit of Happiness." It is perhaps the most recognizable of all declarations regarding freedom. In American Creation (2007) Joseph Ellis, a Mount Holyoke College professor and noted scholar, calls it "the most potent and consequential words in American history" (Ellis, Joseph. American Creation, 2007, p. 56).

Abraham Lincoln considered the Declaration of Independence to be a "statement of principles by which the United States Constitution should be interpreted" (Lincoln. http://www.mrlincolnandthefounders.org/inside.asp?ID=1&subjectID=1)

The Constitution guarantees every individual and corporation (Latin "corpus" means body, i.e. a "legal person") the right to own property, including a business. To use the democracy analogy, consumers "vote" for what they want by deciding which goods and services to buy and at what prices. A product or service continues as long as it receives sufficient "votes." A loss of "votes" might be caused by obsolescence or competition that offers better quality or price. Prices go up or down, based on supply and demand. The motivation for operating a business is the profit an owner receives. Profit is simply the mathematical difference between the production cost and the selling price. Resourceful individuals envision fresh ideas and formulate new and better products and services, which nurtures and advances free enterprise. Capitalism doesn't succeed because of greed. The free market succeeds because it gives people incentive to set aside their own wants and needs in order to address the wants and needs of others. To earn a profit, a business owner must produce goods and services that others are willing to pay for. It is understood that instead of earning a profit, it is possible to incur a loss. This is the essence of financial business risk. It is real and can be substantial. This risk is accepted on the basis that outcomes will be determined solely by the marketplace.

Free enterprise has numerous built-in regulatory checks and balances. One such mechanism is supply and demand. In a competitive market, the unit price of a product or service seeks a price point whereby the quantity demanded by consumers, at the current price, is equal to the quantity supplied by sellers, also at the current price. This results in economic equilibrium. The division of knowledge is another component. If a product uses a particular material, every person whose business relies on that material tracks market changes to adjust manufacturing and pricing, as well as reacting to actions of competitors. Such activity is constant, occurring literally millions, perhaps billions of times every moment of every day. Yet another safeguard is the pricing mechanism. The interchange of supply and demand determines prices, informing both the producers and consumers of the economic equilibrium noted above. It determines allocation of resources, inducing supply to respond to changes in demand.

A short review of pertinent concepts is instructive. First, the link between free enterprise and freedom itself is crucial. Freedom is the "sine qua non" of free enterprise. Sir William

Harcourt, in an 1872 political debate at Oxford, reasoned, "... liberty does not consist in making others do what you think right. The difference between a free Government and a Government which is not free is principally this—that a Government which is not free interferes with everything it can, and a free Government interferes with nothing except what it must."   *The Times* (31 December 1872), p. 5. Without freedom, free enterprise doesn't work. America's founding documents, the Declaration of Independence, the Constitution, and the Bill of Rights are unique in the world. It cannot be overstated that the superior performance of the American free enterprise system relies on this component (Citation: London Times. December 31, 1872. p. 5)

Second, American free enterprise rests on freedom of choice, the freedom of an individual or corporation to own capital goods, to make private investment decisions, and to succeed or fail on the basis of competition in the marketplace. Economic decisions originate in the human mind and are based on supply and demand. Economics is a behavioral science and often unpredictable. Marx was wrong. The insistence of communism and socialist collectivism that economics is subject to the scientific method is simply incorrect. In this respect, free enterprise machinations are similar to those of the U.S. Stock Exchange.

Third, free enterprise has very few operating principles. They are also straightforward. Adam Smith believed the rule of supply and demand, with no adornments, was sufficient to sustain it. Hayek elaborated on this with what he identified as the "Division of Knowledge." This value embodies itself in the infinite number of situations in day-to-day business that hinge on specific knowledge of "time and circumstance." Each instance requires a decision – and an action. In his lectures, Hayek often used the fluctuating price of tin as a typical example. When the price of tin (or any material of production) fluctuates, it sets in motion an incalculable number of decisions for anyone and everyone whose products are in any way affected by the price of tin. These individuals are most likely to have the "knowledge of time and circumstance." When the price increases, there are several choices: a) raise the product price to reflect the increase; b) maintain the product price and absorb the loss; or c) seek alternate material for the affected parts of the product? There are also decisions to be made when the price of tin goes down: a) lower the product price and, if you beat competitors to the market, increase production for a potential windfall; b) retain the product price and risk giving an advantage to the competition. It is inescapable that literally millions upon millions of such decisions occur every minute of every day of every year.

There is also an important caveat. Attempts to intrude and exert centralized control over free enterprise are ill-advised and often disastrous. Endeavors to manipulate the free market system are usually excused as intentions to make the system more "fair" or to "level the playing field." They simply don't work. Free enterprise itself is based on equality for all who participate: worker, owner, investor, and consumer. Free enterprise does not improve with government interference. President Ronald Reagan stated what most of us already know: "Government doesn't fix a problem. Government IS the problem" (Reagan, Ronald. Inaugural Address. January 20, 1981).

The pricing mechanism is significant, because it coordinates the entire free enterprise system. Like a thermometer it reflects current conditions of what is happening across the system. It does not control events. Whenever an attempt is made to control pricing in any way, the most likely outcome is that it will have the opposite effect of the reason for which it was imposed. Going back to the analogy of a thermometer, an attempt to control the pricing system is like expecting the physiological workings of the human body to be controlled by presetting the thermometer. In the first chapter of <u>Basic Economics</u>, Thomas Sowell provides a full discussion of this issue. Any attempt here to do justice to Dr. Sowell's explanation would fail. Sowell's discussion is intended for ordinary citizens not versed in economics. Read it.

Understanding profit and loss hardly takes more than a few words. In the most basic terms, profit is the mathematical difference between production cost and selling price. Loss is negative profit. Contrary to advocates of Marxist economies, profit cannot be a predetermined value. Left alone, it works efficiently.

Freedom & Democracy

In the debate between advocates of free enterprise and a centrally-controlled economy, it does not seem possible to reach a satisfactory conclusion. This is not an objective discussion and the dispute will continue, with advocates of both sides scoring and losing points from time to time.

Free enterprise and its guardians, American freedom and democracy, weren't created and don't sustain themselves at the snap of a finger. They require vision, persistence, and diligence. Some think America is on the cusp of a post-democracy and post-free enterprise era. Those who favor such a transformation constantly chip away at the edges to undermine and discredit the values and principles that shape America's success and prosperity. One of the main arguments is that America's founding ideals and documents are obsolete and in need of revision.

Three - American Entrepreneurism

Freedom is never passé or obsolete and those who believe in "Life, Liberty, and the pursuit of Happiness" must do more than occasionally pledge allegiance to the flag. These values may be viewed by some as "warm" and "fuzzy" ideals to bring out once in a while like prized pets. In fact, they are targets of attack and their preservation requires hard work. To say freedom is not "free," means more than the need to protect America from outside enemies. It can be undermined from within as well.

America's founding fathers were resolute and dogged about their belief in freedom. It is easy to forget that, had the American Revolution not succeeded, King George III would have hanged all the founders and countless more. America's founders were unyielding in their endeavors and persistence to produce a constitutional structure to inspire and harness human creativity and individual initiative. These patriots recognized that free democracy is not a machine of perpetual motion. Once formed, it requires continuing resolve. This legacy is ours and the expectation of America's founders is in our hands. Lazy democracy dies.

Freedom is far too precious and precarious to leave to politicians. Its chief guardians are ordinary citizens and NOT government leaders or the military or wealthy business people. Democracy is at its peak when its practice is focused locally. The greatest peril to Democracy is not found outside America's borders, but inside.

James Madison understood this. In 1788, he stated in Federalist #51: "...you must first enable the government to control the governed; and in the next place oblige it to control itself." Danger lurks, when government, especially at the federal level, grows too large and power becomes concentrated in fewer hands. Local control is the most effective curb against the tendency to centralize governmental functions. This is why the founders delegated so much authority to the individual states. Fiscal policy is another focal point of the checks and balances required for viable democracy. In short, the keys to survival for America's democracy are checks and balances that foster local and smaller government, strong fiscal policies, and effective restraints against fraud and corruption (Madison, James. Federalist #51. 1788).

Don't forget that our American forefathers placed this responsibility in our hands. As Christians, this is another example of the Creator's directive to subdue and have dominion over His creation.

Supporters of free enterprise believe it is a more just and moral economic system. American free enterprise succeeds because it is built on the principles laid out in our founding documents. The greatest of these is freedom and we must never give ground on its exercise of free expression in business or in any other walk of life.

The proof is in the pudding. If we, as advocates of free enterprise and entrepreneurial behavior, wish to prove our answer is the best for America, then we have no choice but to exercise our faith in the free enterprise system and act on our convictions. The objective is not to eliminate anyone. Rather, free enterprise seeks the participation and success of all Americans.

Chapter 3

Discussion Questions

1. How might an economic system help or hinder an entrepreneurial spirit?

2. Discuss the assertion that "the free market succeeds because it gives people incentive to set aside their own wants and needs in order to address the wants and needs of others."

3. How does this emphasis on self-sacrifice impact faith and entrepreneurial action?

4. What does it mean that "Democracy is at its peak when its practice is focused locally"?

5. How is this related to an entrepreneurial life?

Chapter Four

American Exceptionalism

America's free enterprise system has done well. Creativity and initiative have built an economy, society, and polity coveted by the rest of the world. The standard of living for Americans labeled as "poor" is better than that of the middle class in many other countries.

We hear and read about famous entrepreneurs and admire (or envy) their boldness and success. Yet, it is not some small group of outlier geniuses that has made America such an extraordinary country. It was built and continues to prosper mostly because of outwardly unremarkable people. Alexis de Tocqueville, the French political thinker and historian, was so intrigued by the young nation that in 1831 he traveled to America for an extended visit. The trip resulted in his popular book: <u>Democracy in America</u>. The extraordinary character of average citizens and their roles in America's emerging greatness fascinated him. He sensed something special in ordinary citizens of the early 19th Century that was profoundly different from his own countrymen.

De Tocqueville was witnessing the early stages of American Exceptionalism. This phenomenon has evolved into a dynamism that has few boundaries or constraints. It is not limited to persons of European ancestry, the male of our species, or by affluence, or any other demographic attribute. America's DNA pool is populated by a mixture of races, both genders, and all social classes. Certainly, slavery was a dark chapter in America's past. Oppression is as wrong in America as anywhere. The purpose of this book is not to resolve or try to excuse that period of history. Yet, it should be noted that black Americans, despite unimaginable suffering, share the common denominator and inclusiveness of immigrant blood that binds Americans and their ancestors. It seems unlikely that any, given the choice, would return to the repressive rule of a European monarch, Russian czar, African tribal chief, Chinese emperor, communist dictator, Indian rajah, or any other despot.

Ingredients of American Exceptionalism

Creator-Endowed Freedom. What has made America so different? How, why did American Exceptionalism materialize? Proponents argue that it results from a "perfect storm" with three contributing elements. Noted in the previous chapter, the sine qua non (without which, there is none) of the American experiment is freedom. This ingredient was introduced earlier, but bears repeating. This is serious liberty, bequeathed by the Creator and recognized by our founding fathers as the birthright of every American. Such freedom cannot be granted by one human to another. Only God has such omnipotence. It assures every American the "inalienable" right to assemble and speak freely, to come and go at will, to worship according to the voice of conscience, to own private property, to buy and sell as one chooses, to pursue any job and career one desires, to possess and retain financial earnings, and much more.

The significance of Creator-endowed freedom cannot be overstated: neither can we minimize the importance of its recognition by the founders when they gave it such a prominent position in the Declaration of Independence and the Constitution. It is the very heart and spirit of the nation. It is singularly extraordinary, perhaps providential, that these mortals of such faith should assemble in a colonial backwater in the last quarter of the 18th Century to create such a profound progeny. It is equally astonishing that one such as George Washington resisted overwhelming temptation when he was offered the kingship of the new nation. Not any of it, nor what has ensued, could occur without freedom. It doesn't seem likely this was random luck.

Land of Immigrants. The second ingredient in this "stewpot" is the overwhelming preponderance of immigrant blood in America's citizenry. Virtually all Americans have such roots. It is the history of America and American Exceptionalism. These global pilgrims often ventured across unknown oceans at great personal risk to an uncertain destination and future. Our immigrant-ancestors survived by their faith, wits, ingenuity, and stamina. There was no government assistance for new arrivals: no entitlements, no safety nets. They didn't want any. In their countries of origin, government was usually the last source for anything except, perhaps, trouble. Most had few if any earthly goods when they stepped onto the soil of their new homeland. What they did possess, however, was spirit, ambition, and determination to overcome every obstacle. They had indomitable faith in something bigger than themselves and they possessed the will and ability to survive and prosper, if not themselves then their children or their children's children. They demonstrated boundless energy and resolve to work as hard as necessary to make this happen.

An immigrant child married another immigrant child, usually of a similar background. Then their children repeated the process. It is simple and it did not occur by design, but this is the source of the entrepreneurial DNA pool of American Exceptionalism. More than a significant proportion of this unremarkable immigrant group exhibited the two primary traits of entrepreneurs. First and foremost, they were risk-takers who trusted their own instincts and abilities to get things done. Second, they were people of action: self-reliant, undaunted, and indefatigable. They did not want or seek outside assistance. Not only did most survive, many prospered. It can still be seen today, personified, for example, by many of the "boat people" from Viet Nam. They work tirelessly with determination to own their own businesses, even though these may only be small nail salons or convenience stores. This is the open secret of American prosperity.

Much of immigrant literature details the circumstances under which European refugees came to America. We read and know less about other groups, but their sagas are no less dramatic and inspiring. African-Americans came as prisoners on ships that resembled livestock vessels, to be sold as slaves. Yet, their creative and courageous spark could not be denied. They sensed the same image of God as the rest of mankind, knowing that God is colorblind. It seems unlikely that seeing the freedom of their masters would make them long for a return to their ancestral tribes. Instead, it would appear to make them all the more determined to win no less than the freedom they observed. Though it took the Civil War to resolve the issue, virtually all who witnessed their plight, even slave owners, knew the meaning of the words "…all men are created equal". Blacks were heroically engaged in the Civil War, their own American Revolution, with patriotism and passion. The distinguishing entrepreneurial character traits of faith and initiative required to operate the "underground railroad" are undeniable as are the courage and sacrifice of those who fought in the Union Army, though racial discrimination was alive and well in northern states. George Washington Carver is a role model of American Exceptionalism. Perhaps you have read about the

"Buffalo" soldiers, a black U.S. Cavalry troop in the late 1800s. African-Americans line the path of entrepreneurial history and continue today to respond to the directive to subdue and have dominion over the earth.

Tens of millions more have added their own contributions: Chinese were brought to America in circumstances somewhat similar to African-Americans. They were poorly-paid laborers for the railroads, operated laundries, and served as unpaid servants. Russian immigrant history includes a host of persecuted Jewish émigrés. Japanese were virtually imprisoned in internment camps during World War II. The chronicles of the vast majority of American ethnic groups reflect the obstacles and hardships that were ultimately overcome by creativity and drive. The danger that is represented by criminal and illegal drug activity requires strong border security, but we need to be sure legal immigrants continue to be welcomed. It is the key to continued exceptionalism.

Virtually all of us have immigrant roots. Each of us can add the stories that surround the arrival of our ancestors in America. We built and still maintain today what is known as American Exceptionalism. Its chronicles overflow with instance after instance of persons from every race, gender and creed who are the epitome of the servants with five and two talents. The westward expansion that followed the Civil War occurred because ordinary men, women, and families had an entrepreneurial spirit and knew they would succeed by pursuing opportunities in front of them with trust, initiative, and determination to overcome all obstacles. The gravesites that peppered their trails are real, but did not deter them. More recently, World War II evidenced a wealth of entrepreneurial behavior. The industrial machine that supplied the military was run and managed, to a great extent, by wives, mothers, and sisters while their husbands, sons, and brothers fought and won in Asia and Europe. African-American pilots served in their own Army Air Corps (now the U.S. Air Force) Squadron to defend freedom. A squadron of female pilots in the Army Air Corps flew "lend-lease" aircraft from the U.S. to England. A communications unit of Native-Americans protected military intelligence that was transmitted by phone and two-way radio. An Army unit of Japanese-Americans distinguished themselves on the battlefield in Italy.

Individuals of every sort shine in the firmament of American Exceptionalism. It is significant that the vast majority of entrepreneurs do not consider themselves or their deeds to be extraordinary. All possess a common creative trust and positive attitude along with a willingness to work hard. What de Tocqueville witnessed in the 1830s was not the random luck of a lottery jackpot. What he observed is intelligible - and repeatable. It is alive and well today, repeated incessantly in every nook and cranny of the nation, at every moment of every day. What de Tocqueville saw was American Exceptionalism in its raw form.

Entrepreneurial Behavior. The final component in this "perfect storm" is the entrepreneurial character inborn in each of us as part of God's image. It was bestowed at creation and combined with His directive to "subdue and have dominion" over the earth, right where we are. We are not required to travel to another country, speak a different language, or take special training and education. Special circumstances may certainly be part of a person's life and service, but not one of us is excused. No matter what our life situation or circumstances may be, the Creator's directive applies.

As the crown of God's creation we are to constantly be "about our Father's business," in the same way Jesus' parable portrays the servants with five and two talents. When we internalize this, the active use of creative powers and initiative given us in His image comes naturally. God's charge to have dominion over the earth is clarified when Jesus is asked by a lawyer to pinpoint the greatest commandment in Mosaic Law. The answer is simple: love God and love others. The action it requires, however, is anything but easy.

God's gift of His image sets us apart from the rest of the Creator's handiwork in significant ways, of which His interpersonal bond with humans is perhaps the most profound. Recall the scenario in the garden where God came in the "cool of the evening" to talk with Adam and Eve face to face. Although the only instance referenced in Genesis is after humans had fallen victim to the serpent's trap, it is reasonable to assume that such meetings occurred on a regular basis. When humans exercised their freedom to choose the way of the serpent, God did not abandon creation and destroy humanity. Instead, in prototypical entrepreneurial manner and true to His purpose, He enacted an unlikely and unbelievable plan and pathway to return mankind to the relationship. He harbored no regrets for what He had done. He bore no animosity toward His beloved humans, although He was sorely disappointed with their infidelity.

Neither did He remove His image. Major features of that image remain, regardless of the choice to follow the way of the serpent: an immortal soul, freedom, creativity, a relational mind that makes speech and communication possible, to name a few. These traits, discussed in depth in a later chapter, are not retained only by those who have been returned to the relationship with the

73

Creator, but remain active in all humans. So, exactly how are individuals with whom God has restored His interpersonal relationship different from those remaining in the way of the serpent? Obviously, God can discern one from the other, but we need to understand how we are to show the difference in our daily lives.

American Exceptionalism is not some malformed concept of economic Aryanism. It invites and welcomes all, regardless of race, gender, creed, or social class. America's historic "open arms" immigration policy speaks for itself. Not only do we intend to continue feeding this phenomenon to recapture past success, the open invitation to all continues to expand. It is more than difficult to understand those who seek to destroy the reality of American Exceptionalism. Friedrich von Hayek understood it and addressed it in his post-World War II treatise, The Road to Serfdom. Anticipating the importance of post-war economics, he expressed considerable skepticism and warned against too much government control in economic decision-making through central planning. He feared that the loss of individualism and classic liberalism would lead to a loss of freedom, oppression, the tyranny of government control, and the serfdom of individuals. When Readers Digest published an abridged edition in 1945, it became immensely popular. It is still considered a best-seller (Hayek, Friedrich A. The Road to Serfdom. Reader's Digest. April 1945).

American free enterprise exploded following World War II. It continues today. Thanks to the rear view mirror of history, we see without a doubt that it was and is American Exceptionalism.

Chapter 4

Discussion Questions

1. What is "American Exceptionalism" and what is your opinion about whether or not it is a true phenomenon?

2. Discuss the implications of Creator-endowed freedom.

3. The author asserts the formation of an "entrepreneurial DNA pool of American Exceptionalism." What is your opinion about the existence of such a DNA pool?

4. In what significant ways does God's gift of His image set us apart from the rest of the Creator's handiwork?

5. What evidence of American Exceptionalism do you see today?

Chapter Five

Wealth Creation: Resources and the Human Mind

Economic Pie?

The discussion of American Exceptionalism raises the important question of just how wealth is created. To begin with what it is not, the wealth of the American free enterprise economy is not a zero-sum fixed or static amount of money. Unfortunately, the pie metaphor is frequently used to depict the U.S. economy and economic activity. The economic pie is NOT a fixed amount! The pie is NOT owned by society! It is NOT a pie! There is NO pie!

Focusing discussion about wealth on a pie metaphor causes more heat than light, more confusion than enlightenment. First, there is a great misunderstanding and allegation that the economic pie contains a fixed and constant amount of wealth. The assumption that income and wealth in American free enterprise is a zero-sum game leads to a deceptive argument that the rich take most of the pie while the rest get the leftovers. The fact is, the pie is not a pie and it is not constant. The economy, the sum total of goods and services (the would-be pie), is in a state of constant and continuous growth, often at a rapid rate. Only seldom is the growth negative. It is quite likely that even though one's share of the non-existent pie may get smaller, the well-being of that individual improves. A rising tide lifts all ships. At best, the pie metaphor is misleading. At worst, it is purposely deceptive. It is altogether a bad metaphor.

Another misguided notion created by the pie metaphor is an inference that society owns the pie. This concedes a moral point that should *never* be granted. The same charlatans that mislead us, uncertain of just how the pie (wealth) got here, are eager to judiciously divide it "fairly." Wealth does not grow out of some nebulous social process. Collective-society in American democracy does not, in and of itself, collectively own an economic pie. Again, there is NO pie. The notion that "you didn't build that" is completely wrong-headed. That is what Marx asserted. It does not "take a village." What it takes is an individual who accepts the personal risk, trusts his or her own instincts, and is motivated to hard work. These are the entrepreneurial traits, identified earlier, that lead to wealth creation.

Natural Resources

Some believe wealth creation is proportional to the availability of resources found in nature. Certainly, natural resources can enhance wealth creation. Yet, if the presence of natural resources is the key component, what can explain the historic poverty found in Russia, which has vastly more such resources than virtually any other country, including America. What about the wealth of Singapore? The Island of Singapore is a "tiny red dot" on the map, as a Malaysian leader once ridiculed. It is approximately 27 miles long and 15 miles wide with over 5 million people. It has NO natural resources, except its people. Yet, its wealth index is one of the highest in the world. Among various wealth measures, Singapore has the highest per capita ownership of Mercedes Benz automobiles in the world.

Creation of Wealth

There is no doubt that the variety and abundance of natural resources are important to America. Commodities such as coal, crude oil, iron ore, precious metals, and uranium play a key role in the country's prosperity. The question, however, is whether or not in and of themselves they are direct causes of America's wealth. To answer, think about where, how, and when these resources are isolated, harvested, and used. Only with the addition of a catalyst is matter transformed into useful and valuable products. That critical reactive agent is the human mind, the ultimate natural resource. Cellphones are not dug up from some mine deep in the earth. Computers aren't found hidden behind cacti in the desert. The space shuttle wasn't given to us by some asteroid in space. Earthly wealth flows from the human mind. Nothing becomes a natural resource until a human mind figures out how to use it in a worthwhile way to improve our lives. Prior to that, it is not a resource. Mentioned earlier, the early inhabitants of Pennsylvania found black ooze coming out of the ground. Though there is evidence early American Indians used the crude oil for limited medicinal purposes, it spoiled land that could otherwise have been used for farming or hunting. It became useful only when the human mind formulated petro-chemical processes and built on countless separate insights, one step at a time, to discover uses of crude oil for the benefit of all. Many materials we consider to be natural resources would still be in the ground, likely considered useless, except for human creativity and initiative

(Paleontological Research Institute, "The Story of Oil in Pennsylvania,"

http://www.priweb.org/ed/pgws/history/pennsylvania/pennsylvania.html).

In the purely secular world, wealth is created and morally belongs to the individual who created it. Much the same was taught by such as the writer of Aesop's Fables in the story of the ant and the grasshopper. The grasshopper enjoys life during the summertime when it is warm and food is in ample supply, while the ant works industriously to prepare for winter. It was told to impress youth with the importance of work and frugality. Dee Howard, who founded the Dee Howard Aircraft Company, left school after 9th grade when his father died and he had to help sustain his family. He was a bright young man and fascinated with the emerging field of aeronautics. In his lifetime, he received more than 50 patents, mostly aeronautical inventions. He made and lost several fortunes during his lifetime. His inventions created wealth for himself and others. The credit for what he did could not be claimed by someone who worked for him on the basis that it was really laborers who created his wealth. Society could not make the claim either. Yet, all of us continue to benefit from his inventions and the resulting products that improve lives. The direct benefits rightly should have and did accrue to Dee Howard. The next time you are watching a private jet aircraft that uses thrust reversers to slow its landing speed, think of Dee Howard. He did that, not workers, not society, and not government. That is wealth creation.

There is a pertinent and true story, told by the unidentified author of the "Coyote Blog" website. (Cited with permission.) I will paraphrase it. The author was in an intense discussion about economics with a university student whose knowledge of economics had been shaped primarily by faculty of a progressive persuasion. "Coyote" started the discussion by issuing the following challenge. Sand is almost pure silica, so take this handful of sand (they were sitting at the beach) and produce a computer. There are several ground-rules. First, assume you have however much money you need. Second, you may use as much manual labor and laborers as you wish, but only manual labor. You may not use engineers, designers, managers, or providers of other knowledge or business services. Third, you may purchase and use as much material as you wish, but only in its natural and unrefined state: land and timber, but not buildings; iron ore, but not steel; sand, but not silicon; flowing water, but not electricity.

The student was stumped. The task is impossible until a person rationalizes and fabricates raw materials into useable components. Then another person must design and assemble the finished product. The difference between sand that is worth virtually nothing and microchips that are worth thousands of dollars per gram is the value that human minds have added.

It was not until the life of economist Julian Simon (1932-1998) that the concept of the human mind as the ultimate resource was crystalized. Simon concluded: "The ultimate resource is people – especially skilled, spirited, and hopeful young people endowed with liberty – who will exert their wills and imaginations for their own benefit, and so inevitably benefit not only themselves but the rest of us as well" (Simon, Julian, *The Ultimate Resource 2*, Princeton, N.Y.: Princeton University Press, 1996, p. 581. Also: http://www.masterresource.org/2014/07/simon-ultimate-resource/#sthash.JvYtqJPg.dpuf).

Wealth of the World

At the time of the American Revolution, the vast majority of the world's wealth was vested in land. Only a very small part of the rest was in early forms of wealth creation. Mainly, the world's wealth was fixed: stable and unchanging. Transfer of wealth occurred almost exclusively by inheritance. The exception, precious metals and gems, derived value from scarcity, not utility.

Today, the percentage is reversed, with as much as 90% of affluence in the U.S. emanating predominantly from creative and hard-working middle class Americans who use their minds and hands to create new products. Until recently, most new products came from matter found on or in the earth, such as crude oil, timber, and iron ore. These raw materials were processed into useful form, like gasoline, lumber, and steel, or shaped into components for assembly in factories. There has always been a group of products that emanate from the cerebral cortex. They are referred to as the Arts, but are not normally thought of as products in the marketplace. Today, we are in the information age. As this industry advances, the percentage of material components is decreasing and the amount of mental processing is increasing. Technology and software products use fewer tangible components. Increasingly, products contain "knowledge" components, such as discs with data in digital form or software, purchased, downloaded, and transferred via the Internet.

How did we get from a world of fixed wealth (the pie, again) to a situation in which wealth is in a constant and explosive state of growth and flux, usually positive? What has changed? The primary alteration has been the acquisition of freedom. From the beginning of recorded history, mankind has struggled to gain freedom. It moved at a snail's pace with important advances from time to time like the Code of Hammurabi, the Ten Commandments, the Roman Senate, and the Magna Carta. It took a final leap when America's founders declared freedom for all in 1776.

Freedom is accompanied by two critical conditions on which the creation of wealth is dependent. First, it confers the right to question and challenge authority, established beliefs, superstitions, and social patterns. Second, it enables individuals to learn (first characteristic of entrepreneurs) and to use their own initiative (second characteristic of entrepreneurs) to pursue ideas and retain the rewards, monetary and otherwise.

Some fault religious strictures for backwardness that plagues and restrains humanity. Certainly, some early belief systems thwarted attempts at freedom of thought and action. In truth, however, it is often groups of pious people, particularly America's founding fathers, who have the vision (first characteristic) and pursue actions (second characteristic) that address problems of society ranging from the birthing of a nation to mundane issues like sanitation, bureaucratic structure, civil order, formalized learning, and commercial trade. It should be noted that the way of the serpent is itself a "religion", whose object of worship is every person as their own god. The prohibitions of this belief system are especially dehumanizing and destructive. In fact, the height of tyranny and "man's inhumanity to man" is the very essence of repression and oppression. Only when religion takes on the trappings of the way of the serpent does it fall into the trap of shackling humans. Why would any independently thinking person (to think is to engage the very image of God we have been given) purposely give or allow a ruler the authority to take away the most precious gift of freedom? A ruler who takes away freedom does so purely to exert greed and power over others.

The free market dramatically changes lives all over the world. Wherever you find freedom to exert creativity and initiative (the two conditions noted above) you also find growth, increasing wealth, and advancing standards of living. At the end of Mao Zedong's tyrannical rule and the ascendency of Dong Xiaoping, Chinese peasants were given the opportunity to sell and keep the profits from excess produce, after fulfilling the required quota for their collective. Some estimate that this "market economy" venture effectively doubled production for several years. Over the past two decades, hundreds of millions of people, including 400 million Chinese, have left the ranks of poverty, one of the greatest socio-economic movements in the history of the world.

Wherever the two conditions are not found, poverty and misery continue to breed their own "clones". It is all that can exist in such an environment. Four billion people, two-thirds of the world, do not have freedom to create thriving markets. It is these repressive governments that imprison minds and restrain progress, not Christianity. Limiting their citizens condemns their own countries. Why? It is the serpent telling those who are and seek to remain in power, "Ye shall be as gods." His message is to stay in control, no matter what it takes. No one will notice the misuse and abuse of power. If people object, ignore it.

Evil does exist. There is much evil in the world. Freedom and God go hand in hand. One does not exist without the other.

Where the two conditions exist the future is bright, for the ultimate natural resource is the human mind. It is, perhaps, the only true natural resource. By this reasoning, only the smallest fraction of physical natural resources has been uncovered and harnessed. The greatest likelihood in this scenario is that entrepreneurial startups will increase exponentially, both in number and rate. As individuals work and are informed by the Internet, other knowledge sources, and communication devices, they will constantly create new and innovative products, including many in developing countries. Learning is becoming more self-directed. Without substantial adjustments to the education and learning process, in fact, the "death knell" for traditional academic institutions may be tolling already. Imagine millions of people with cell phones that are also computing devices. Electronic creative expression is changing the way we think of creative arts. The written word will compete with the performing and visual arts. The potential is limitless. The ultimate natural resource is the human mind and people who are full of faith, inspired, and unafraid of hard work. Their imagination and initiative benefit all of humanity. The upshot and wonderful irony of this natural resource is that its use does not deplete it. Instead, as it is utilized it expands. Who would ever have created such magnificence? Who would ever give up such freedom?

Chapter 5

Discussion Questions

1. What is the "economic pie" and how does the concept impact entrepreneurial action?

2. Why is the relationship between individual action and wealth creation important?

3. Discuss the notion that "the ultimate resource is people." How does this impact your day-to-day values and action?

4. What thoughts and responses do you have about the following paragraph:
   "Freedom is accompanied by two critical conditions on which the creation of wealth is dependent. First, it confers the right to question and challenge authority, established beliefs, superstitions, and social patterns. Second, it enables individuals to learn (first characteristic of entrepreneurs) and to use their own initiative (second characteristic of entrepreneurs) to pursue ideas and retain the rewards, monetary and otherwise."

5. What impact do you believe technology will have on entrepreneurial development?

Chapter Six

Right Side Up or Upside Down

The innocence and freedom of life in the garden was not a libertarian existence. Work was an expression of oneness with the Creator and there was a recognized code of behavior:

"...You are free to eat from any tree in the garden; but you must not eat from the tree of the knowledge of good and evil, for when you eat of it you will surely die." (Genesis 2:16-17 NIV)

When the serpent convinced the humans to serve themselves, God's threat of death became a reality. Yet, neither the serpent nor the humans foresaw God's next move. It was forgiveness and it came, as we say, "out of the blue." Who would ever create such a radical and entrepreneurial action plan as this? It is no wonder He is God and we are not! God is love. He is also the power to forgive. That is true omnipotence! It is the same creativity and initiative we are to use as we carry out the Creator's directive in our own lives.

Regardless of the mutiny of the first humans, major features of God's image remain. Yet, those with whom God has restored His relationship are fundamentally different from those remaining in the way of the serpent. Obviously, the Creator can distinguish one from the other, but how can we know? More importantly, how should this knowledge alter our daily lives?

Those restored to the relationship with the Creator experience a parallel change in behavior: *"Be holy because I, the*

LORD *your God, am holy." (Leviticus 19:2 NIV)* It applies no less in our day than when first uttered. The shift is a sea change that strikes at our inner being. You can feel it. It has to do with the transformed motivation from which our actions flow. It is the inspiration and stimulus that caused the servants with five and two talents to enact what their master had instilled in them. It is an entrepreneurial faith and action by which we are motivated. It returns us to the garden, where the Creator tasked the humans to subdue and have dominion.

Early Christians were accused of inverting human reality. The King James Version captures the essence: *"...These that have turned the world upside down are come hither also;" (Acts 17:6 KJV).* In fact, however, their actions reflected human existence and behavior as the Creator originally intended. It is life in the way of the serpent that is upside down.

Upside Down World

The difference is a direct contrast to the self-centered behavior of humans as their own gods. Happily, we are not left alone to figure it out for ourselves. God's Word informs and instructs us. Among the most significant teaching sessions is Jesus' "Sermon on the Mount" that includes a subset called the Beatitudes. Almost all Christians have heard of the Beatitudes and most likely have read them, perhaps more than once. Some may even have memorized them. Understanding and using them in our daily lives, however, is an arduous challenge. They typically receive scant attention in Christian instruction. Two issues come to mind. First, the Beatitudes are really harsh medicine. Many consider them impossible to enact. Second, they seem to suggest weakness as the posture for those who follow the way of the Lord.

Without realizing it, these views show that we are still in the grip of the serpent, trapped by upside down reasoning.

The World Upside Down: or Right Side Up, a small but powerful book by Paul G. Bretscher, speaks directly to this and provides a breakthrough understanding of the Beatitudes. His prologue explains the difficulty with a story about an individual fitted with special eyeglasses that inverted all images similar to what you see under the hood of an old-fashioned portrait camera. At first it was extremely difficult to navigate, but the person eventually adapted to this upside down world. The story has a basis in fact. Such an experimental study, with the same outcome, was conducted by George M. Stratton in the 1890s. It is an excellent metaphor for precisely what happened when humans chose the way of the serpent (Bretscher, Paul G. The World Upside Down: or Right Side Up. 1964. St. Louis. Concordia Publishing House, and: George M. Stratton. Some preliminary experiments on vision, *Psychological Review*, 1896).

The Creator's right side up world has been radically distorted by the way of the serpent, to the point that right is seen as wrong and wrong as right. Truth is the main victim. It has mutated into a relative term. We are told that "it all depends." Depends on what? Countless examples show us how the way of the serpent has altered God's truth. Marriage, the only statute ordained by God before mankind incarcerated itself in the way of the serpent, is hard to recognize. Many dismiss it and live together until one becomes tired or bored with the other and they split up, as if nothing happened. Daily, from our elected leaders down to the least of us, we witness deceit, larceny, sexual escapades, fraud, insider trading, and virtually any other wrongdoing you might choose. Perhaps the most blatant is abortion. Annually, it "legally" ends the lives of more than a million Americans. It is not recognized for the butchery that it is. In the fairly recent past, such action was treated as homicide, premeditated at that.

These human failures have a common denominator. They can all be traced back to a breakdown of relationships. Jesus and His Father, our Father, understand this. Jesus bluntly declares God's right side up truth in the Beatitudes. He gives no quarter and refuses to accept or cave in to what is considered socially refined or politically correct. He doesn't just preach about the Beatitudes, He lives them with the same entrepreneurial behavior as the Creator and Father who sent Him. In the process it cost Him His life. His death, however, gave back the life every one of us had lost.

In truth, the Beatitudes call for anything but weakness. When Jesus' disciples were arguing over who was the greatest, He used a child, who was weak in the eyes of the upside down world, for His object lesson:

"...I tell you the truth, unless you change and become like little children, you will never enter the kingdom of heaven" (Matthew 18:3 NIV).

What we may not comprehend is that true weakness is the opposite and upside down way of the serpent. Its self-centeredness condemns humanity to eternal separation from God. The Beatitudes are in direct contrast and represent a position of authentic strength. The reward for this behavior is the inheritance of earth and heaven. Bretscher's framework contrasts the right side up way of the Lord with the upside down way of the serpent.

- Dignity. Blessed are the poor in spirit, for theirs is the kingdom of heaven.

Upside down: Blessed are those whose spirits are high, for they sit on top of the world.

- Joy. Blessed are those who mourn, for they shall be comforted.
Upside down: Blessed are those who refuse to mourn, for they need no comfort.

- Security. Blessed are the meek, for they shall inherit the earth.
Upside down: Blessed are the aggressive, for they shall dominate the earth.

- Ambition. Blessed are those who hunger and thirst for righteousness, for they shall be satisfied.
Upside down: Blessed are those who are satisfied with their righteousness, for there are more important things to hunger for.

- Justice. Blessed are the merciful, for they shall obtain mercy.
Upside down: Blessed are those who have rights, for they shall obtain justice.

- Wisdom. Blessed are the pure in heart, for they shall see God.
Upside down: Blessed are the sharp of mind, for they "can't see" God.

- Peace. Blessed are the peacemakers, for they shall be called the sons of God.

Upside down: Blessed are those who dictate the peace, for they shall play the role of God.

- Conformity. Blessed are those who are persecuted for righteousness' sake, for theirs is the kingdom of heaven.

  Blessed are you when men revile you and persecute you and utter all kinds of evil against you falsely on my account. Rejoice and be glad, for your reward is great in heaven, for so men persecuted the prophets who were before you.

  Upside down: Blessed are those who are accepted for being so agreeable, for they sit on top of the world.

  Blessed are you when men like you, accept you, want you for their leader, and consider themselves fortunate to know you. Rejoice and be flattered, for great is your prestige on earth; for so men have accepted the conformists who were before you (Ibid, Bretscher, pp 4-5).

The strength of the Beatitudes is found in their focus on God's directive to subdue and have dominion over His creation. Only when we get beyond the self-centered desire and fear of the tree of the knowledge of good and evil are we able to relate Jesus' teaching to our own lives. An understanding begins to emerge as we recognize that they call for behavior that is God-centered and other person-centered.

The Son was sent into a world that was upside down to God's posture because of the alienation that occurred when mankind opted for the false promise of the serpent. Yet, Jesus was the one accused of being upside down. In truth, He walked in a right side up relationship with the Father as was expected of mankind from the beginning. At best Jesus was deemed odd, out of step, and perverse. At worst He was regarded naïve and unruly, a potential threat to the control exerted by religious leaders of the day. In the Beatitudes Jesus declares God's love for mankind and His desire for all to return to the right side up interpersonal bond with God, established at creation. The way of the Lord is a surprising path, at times even to those who claim to be believers. The behavior to which Jesus points is in direct opposition to the self-centered way of the serpent. It is not difficult to understand, but impossible to do unless we become re-connected to our Maker by being clothed in the actions of the Son. The way of the Lord is counterintuitive and upside down to the way of the serpent. Yet, it is the only right side up posture. Lose your life to find it. Love God and love your fellowman. Not a word about me, self, pride, power, control, and everything else the upside down world pursues.

Entrepreneurial Dominion

To repeat an earlier question: what separates those God has brought back into relationship with Himself from those still ensnared in the way of the serpent? The serpent tethers us like leashed pets, but in reality he is not as clever as we are gullible. The serpent leads with seemingly minor issues and then progresses to more important matters. Practical and ordinary concerns nag at us. The recent exchange with an unemployed friend is revealing. A person of faith, he believes God guides his life and cares for him. He knows and understands Jesus' mandate to serve God and his fellowman, but he is tortured by this personal predicament, namely taking care of himself and his family. Trusting and serving God and his fellowman is fine, but he must first find a job, right?

Dealing with such circumstances is a Catch-22 quandary, but it is also upside down thinking. Of course, my friend should seek employment with energy and determination. That's not the issue. The concern is motive and attitude. The serpent has convinced us that outcome is all that matters and the way we resolve challenges is of no consequence. It is the other way around. Jesus paints a bull's-eye on the self-love at the heart of the way of the serpent. He places us right back in the garden. Are we god or is God? If we are god then our only option is to live according to the tree of the knowledge of good and evil, the way of the serpent. Humans as god live by lust and desire for whatever it wants, or in dread and avoidance of everything unwanted. It is the behavior we observe in nature. By falling for the way of the serpent, we plunge ourselves into the upside down world of survival of the fittest. In the process, we abuse each other as well as the rest of God's creation to the point that there is no dignity, no joy, no security, no realized ambition, no justice, no wisdom, and no peace.

There are other facets. At first glance, God's directive to have dominion over the earth clashes and is incompatible with the behavior called for in the Beatitudes. The confusion stems from the upside down view and attitude of the way of the serpent that sees Beatitude-behavior as not only weak, but also irrational. Only after we are turned right side up are we able to grasp its potency. "Love God and love your neighbor" is filled with power. It is the way of the Lord and anything but foolish or feeble.

God's alternate plan flips us back to His right side up world. Don't concentrate on not sinning. That is self-centered and you can't win that battle. Rather, focus on Jesus' proactive answer to concentrate our lives on loving God and our fellowmen. It is notable that "self" is not part of His fiat. Not in a single, solitary place does Scripture sanction love of self. In fact, Jesus' counsel goes the other direction:

"If anyone would come after me, he must deny himself...whoever wants to save his life will lose it, but whoever loses his life for me will find it." (Matthew 16:24 NIV)

Denying oneself does not mean self-abuse, for that is no more than violence against one's own body. Besides being wrong, it is still attention to self. Rather, we are to focus on honoring our Creator and our fellowmen. It is the serpent who deceives us into rationalizing self-love. His logic informs me that if I am god then I am also the most important person. Everyone else is in second place, or lower. It doesn't work!

God's charge incorporates a dual strategy. First, we are to subdue and exercise dominion over the earth, i.e., serve God and neighbor. Second, we are to carry this out from a right side up posture. That's it! Use the gift of God's image to create. The Creator gave us His image because He delights in our use of that capacity. That is the motivation and initiative of the servants with five and two talents. It is entrepreneurial and imitates the model-behavior of the Master.

The demeanor of the rich fool is self-centered pride and arrogance. He gives zero thought to God and anyone else, preoccupied with lust and greed for whatever he desires or dread and avoidance of what he fears. His motives and actions are contradictory to Jesus' answer about God's pivotal commandment. If the fool does occasionally show a level of charitable behavior, it likely occurs when he knows others are watching and he feels pressured. Not only is his action a pretense, he resents it. In his upside down world everything is for sale and anything can be bought. It is all an economic exchange and he has the money. The behavior of the servant with one talent appears to be different, but

95

displays the same self-serving motive. Lust and fear are served by idleness. He does nothing, expecting and even demanding that others provide for his needs and comfort. After all, it is not his fault that he has less than others. According to him and the upside down power structure, he deserves a fair and guaranteed income so he can enjoy the same "creature comforts" as those with more. In addition, he should be given free housing, free healthcare, free retirement, and everything else enjoyed by the rich.

There is tragic irony, perhaps even dark humor, in the self-serving behavior of the rich fool and the servant with one talent, as well as all who remain in the way of the serpent. Without realizing it, the rich fool pits himself against everything and everyone, but especially against God. It is an endless live-or-die battle, i.e., survival of the fittest. This term originated in evolutionary theory, but the conflict has been going on since the moment the serpent duped humans into thinking they can be their own gods. The lazy servant has found a different niche. Filled with self-pity, he acts out a role that allows those in upside down positions to justify ungodly and unhealthy control of the lives of others. Mankind is in way over its head. The only engagement mustered is to wage a battle it shouldn't even be fighting.

The serpent sees it and laughs, for the simpleton would-be man-god doesn't comprehend that he has been relegated to the level of plants and animals. Do you think the serpent is the friend of humans? Friendship is a blessing received as part of God's image. The serpent doesn't have that capacity. He makes a pretense of friendship only to draw people deeper into his prison of deceit. There are no friends in hell. Like the Coachman in the story of "Pinocchio", the serpent uses "candy" and "toys" to stir desire that ends in imprisonment. This is the essence of the tree of the knowledge of good and evil. The serpent manipulates us by lust to pursue whatever we desire. That's the "good" from the tree. The obverse, "evil", drives us with anxiety to avoid whatever we don't want. How pathetic. These are animal instincts. The lust to have whatever appears as desirable and to avoid anything perceived as evil is the stark reality of those determined to be gods. Beyond this, mankind compounds error with error by misusing the vestige of the unearned and undeserved gift of the image of God to abuse the earth and subjugate other humans, often in a violent fashion. Finally, using faulty reasoning and abetted by the serpent, mankind concludes that the serpent himself does not exist (could the serpent be any more self-serving?) and there is only an "empty blank" after death. What possesses a person to choose this instead of being the heir of earth and heaven? It is truly beyond understanding. It is truly upside down.

The third type of behavior is exemplified by the servants with five and two talents: positive and to the point. They grasp God's truth, focusing all their attention and behavior outside themselves, i.e., on their Master and fellowman. They carry out the Master's charge in a way that exercises dominion over the earth and at the same time is perfectly aligned with Jesus' admonitions in the Beatitudes. The scope of the parable encompasses much more than money or business matters. It stretches across all aspects of life: family, career, social, moral, economic, and psychological, but especially the interpersonal relationship with the Master, who is God. The creativity and personal drive they bring to the task might be described as mustard seed-faith joined with relentless action, the two uncompromising traits of entrepreneurs. This flies in the face of the upside down world's reason and conventional wisdom. The Master calls them good and faithful. They accomplish all the Master intends.

The two servants are not exempt from the effects of the tree of the knowledge of good and evil. Everyone must deal with these issues every day. In fact, they undoubtedly get more attention and temptation from the serpent than those already under his sway. The difference is that rather than "taking" what they desire and "rejecting" what is repugnant, they live their lives by "giving and receiving." This is part of the training received from their master. It is precisely the behavior exhibited by Jesus during His time on earth. We may understand and appreciate the importance of giving to our fellowmen, but what might we give to God as He has everything already? This is upside down thinking. The gift God wants is simple thanksgiving and praise for what we receive from Him. He delights in giving us all things and He delights in our thankful response.

The action of "taking" is instigated by the tree of the knowledge of good and evil, authored by the way of the serpent. "Rejecting" has the same source. "Giving and Receiving", on the other hand, are actions of the Creator. "Giving" is easy enough for us to comprehend: it is the action of giving something of yours to someone else. It was God's creation action. "Receiving", however, has a curious twist. Receiving the "good" is easy and we are happy to do so. Are we to receive "evil" as well? Can this possibly mean what it says? Again, look at Jesus and His behavior. How did He respond when "evil" is what He received? In short, He simply received it. A suffering Job makes a pertinent observation: *"Shall we accept good from God, and not trouble?" (Job 2:10 NIV)*. Look back to the beginning, for it is more striking. Picture the Creator completing creation by giving humans His image as well as the universe. Humans respond by rejecting the entire gift. In short, this is pure "evil" being received by the Creator. We are astonished, but that is because our view is upside down, derived from the tree of the knowledge of good and evil. God received ungrateful and repugnant behavior from the crown of His creation. He didn't suddenly decide to add the consequence of punishment after man chose the way of the serpent. It was a part of the original condition God set when man was placed in the garden. Beyond that, He does nothing. That's it. He simply receives man's disobedience. Then He gives again. The gift is His Son. It brings us back. This surely seems upside down, but its right side up behavior, pure and perfect entrepreneurism.

Chapter 6

Discussion Questions

1. Discuss the creativity involved in God's plan of salvation for humanity.

2. What major features of God's image remain in humanity?

3. How do these impact our life and action?

4. What stands out to you most as you read about "the right side up way of the Lord" as summarized in the Beatitudes?

5. Discuss how Jesus personified the entrepreneurial "right side up" life God intends.

Chapter Seven

The Mandate: Serve God, Serve Others

Right side up behavior revealed in the Beatitudes reiterates God's directive to subdue and have dominion over creation. It is summarized in the Two Tables of the Law: we are to abandon the self-centered way of the serpent to serve God and our fellowman. Such conduct is not doable as long as we are imprisoned in the upside down way of the serpent. We don't want to or even think to act in such manner. With joy and gratitude, we can only thank our Creator God that the last Adam has reconciled and returned us to the relationship we had in the beginning, right side up. It isn't easy. On our own, it's not even possible. Further, we regularly revert to a comfortable upside down attitude. Thankfully, we are brought back each time by God's Grace to entrepreneurial right side up lives by an entrepreneurial God.

Blessed are the poor in spirit for theirs is the kingdom of heaven.

This may be the most significant of the Beatitudes. The rest seem to flow from it. It concerns self-worth and was the only issue broached by the serpent in the garden. Although the humans knew they had the image of God, the serpent shrewdly turned it upside down. He appealed to their ego, suggesting they could improve their position by their own will. A thin line separates self-confidence and vanity. Unfortunately for humans, the power for them to create self-worth was not included in the gifts they received from the Creator's image. God holds that to Himself.

Certainly, God knows the importance of dignity. Individual worth is part of His creation gift. It takes an entrepreneurial mindset, however, to understand this quality of God's image. Accepted by faith (first entrepreneurial trait), it is the driving force (second trait) in the lives of those who follow the way of the Lord. Jesus didn't concern Himself with personal worth. St. Paul tells us that Jesus *"...being in very nature God, did not consider equality with God something to be grasped." (Philippians 2:6 NIV)* Jesus did not feel threatened or compelled to hold on to His divinity to know it was real. He trusted the Father's Word and freely set it aside to take human form so God's Plan could be enacted. He knew He was Son and Heir and didn't need additional proof. Neither should we. Each of us was named an heir and restored to that position, thanks to Jesus. God's free gift of dignity is infinitely superior to the "clay feet" of attempts by humans to create their own self-worth.

There is a special pearl of wisdom in the parable of the talents. Any notion that you may be less capable than others is an errant assumption that comes from the way of the serpent. This is what the servant with one talent thought. Rather than rejoice in his talent and apply the lessons and tutelage of his master, he determined his was of less value than those of his fellow servants. His gift wasn't less important, but merely different. Why should he, or we, shun the talent we receive? Instead, our response is to be one of creativity and initiative to develop it to its maximum potential. We don't have to prove our worth. We need only to focus on the gift received and God's trust in us. God's image gives each of us a complete and separate identity. Don't allow yourself to be talked out of believing in your unique standing as a child of the King. When we subordinate ourselves to others, it belittles what God has done for each of us. Your talent is the Creator's gift to you. Make it all He intends. That's the power of God's image. Don't plug yourself into the success formula of someone else. The

Image of God is not composed in monotonous imitations of the creative process. Like the servants with five and two talents, the Master deals with us on the basis of the talent we receive and how we increase it, not by comparing us with others.

Steve Jobs is recognized as one of America's premier entrepreneurs. His understanding of individual creativity and initiative was extraordinary. In 2005 he told the Stanford graduating class, "Your time is limited, so don't waste it living someone else's life. Don't be trapped by dogma – which is living with the results of other people's thinking. Don't let the noise of others' opinions drown out your own inner voice. And most important, have the courage to follow your heart and intuition." Don't assume anyone is smarter than you. Don't hide behind the excuse that you can't succeed because other people have more talent. That is an evasion and a really bad one, at that. Never assume you are inferior, not as creative, or not as valid.

Don't question your worth. That is taken care of. You are God's child and heir. Move the focus of worship off of yourself. Concentrate attention on thanksgiving toward the Creator and help your fellowmen understand and grasp that the best way to fulfill God's expectations is by serving Him and each other. That is the entrepreneurial meaning of dignity.

Blessed are those who mourn, for they shall be comforted.

Why mourn? At first glance, it doesn't appear to fit the lexicon of entrepreneurial behavior and it certainly is not welcome in the self-centered way of the serpent. This is why: sin is real, death is real, and judgment is real. Un-real is the serpent's fabrication and fantasy that a self-centered life is the norm to be sought. Death is horrifying. A corpse rots and stinks. It is put into the ground or cremated as soon as possible and forgotten. Everyone meets the same earthly fate, but for those ensnared in the way of the serpent, the end of this life is a portal to spiritual and eternal death. Although we do not know the reality of total and eternal separation from God, we have clues. Jesus referred to it as *"weeping and gnashing of teeth."* The word gnash comes from Greek, the language of the New Testament, and means "to bite," like wild dogs gnashing their teeth on each other over a carcass. When love of God and fellowman is gone, what remains is only hatred and envy. It is not possible to imagine and understand the utter panic, horror, and terror of permanent separation from God.

To mourn is to acknowledge and own this awful truth. We cannot reverse it or its consequences. The response witnessed in the person and life of Jesus is utter nonsense to the upside down world. He singles out mourners, those in anguish of their sins. He forgives them. How entrepreneurial! Jesus mourned at Lazarus' grave and over the City of Jerusalem. In Gethsemane, He was gripped by the horror of death, sweated blood, and pled with His Father to find another way.

Recognize God's judgment against rebellion: the pride, arrogance, greed, and bitter resistance of mankind, the Crown of Creation. Then mourn. That is precisely His command. Jesus hung on the cross, mourning not for Himself, but for us. He died. Don't be afraid to mourn with Him, for it has an entrepreneurial outcome. Believe the empty tomb and receive His promise. Our response is just as entrepreneurial as His sacrifice, for it is His power, not ours, that bridges the chasm. It can be explained, but never understood. Our mourning is turned to comfort, thanksgiving, and joy. We are to share this fantastic news in all we do and say. It is not philosophy or fantasy, but history and reality, as God intended it. It is God's Plan. He returns us to Himself in a perfect and eternal relationship, as intended from the beginning.

Blessed are the meek, for they shall inherit the earth.

In the upside down world of the serpent, nothing Jesus said is more patently ludicrous than the notion that meekness is blessed. Like the rich fool, those in the way of the serpent find security in material and intellectual possessions, especially in the power they amass. In the upside down world, meekness is weakness. Lyrics from Camelot, a Broadway musical, convey the view: "it's not the earth the meek inherit, it's the dirt." It is revealing how easily mankind is manipulated into lowering itself to the instinct level of animals. The inability to resist exploitation and degradation proves our naiveté, gullibility, and vulnerability and precludes attainment of the security we seek. How easily we are lead down any false path baited with his lies. There is one truth of God's Word, but the way of the serpent offers limitless other routes. The upside down quest for security is a bumpy ride. It cannot be taken and held, for when it seems certain then something pops up to reveal yet another weakness or failing. Then we die. Judgment follows.

To be sure, there is nothing wrong with earthly riches. Abraham was wealthy and God was the source. There is no condemnation of wealth created by entrepreneurs like Steve Jobs, Bill Gates, Sam Walton, and untold millions more. Creation of phenomenal wealth does not make one an enemy of God. In fact, they are using gifts of the image of God the way He intends. The snag is in attitude and motivation.

Why the dilemma? God promised: *"...seek first His kingdom and His righteousness, and all these things will be given to you as well". (Matthew 7:33 NIV)* Isn't that enough? Do we require something we can see and touch? Faith does not rely on tangible means. Jesus noted that wild animals have a nest or den, but the Son of Man didn't even have a pillow on which to lay His head. Yet, He was secure in the relationship with His Father. The response to His earthly condition was an entrepreneurial "so what?" learned from His Father. He knew and believed the promise of His inheritance. So should we.

Humility characterized in this Beatitude doesn't mean what the upside down world thinks. The meek are neither cowards nor weak. The upside down world can't understand there is no need for the meek to attain control over the world's "stuff". It is already theirs, a part of the birthright as the King's heirs. We also understand, however, that none of this is our own doing. Like the servants with five and two talents, we use the power embedded in the Creator's entrepreneurial directive to have dominion over His earth and, make no mistake, it is His earth. Those whom He has returned to a relationship with Himself have no reason to be timid about using the full extent of resources given by God, particularly those embodied in His image and fixed in us at creation. It is God's intent and purpose that we manifest in our resourcefulness and control over the earth the very creativeness of God, Whose Spirit breathes in us.

There are two unspoken proscriptions not to bring harm, environmentally or otherwise, to His creation. Beware, for the serpent uses God's directive to dominate the earth as opportunity to contaminate meekness with pride and to pervert creativity into sin. The first injunction is against any attempt to subdue God. The second is against the domination of other people. These two are the principal sins of humanity. All others fall within their boundaries. Jesus' admonition to the disdainful lawyer stated them in entrepreneurial terms: *"Love the Lord your God with all your heart and with all your soul and with all your mind...and...love your neighbor as yourself." (Matthew 22:37-39 NIV)* Create strategies and actions to fulfill and enjoy the security promised in this Beatitude.

Blessed are those who hunger and thirst for righteousness, for they shall be satisfied.

It is not possible for two worlds to have a more polar difference. It is also difficult to imagine something so insignificant and infinitesimally small as faith to be the lifeline that brings us back from the abyss of the way of the serpent. Jesus even compares it to a mustard seed. What is not small is God's grace, Christ on the cross, an invitation to participate in the relationship offered by God, and the promise to inherit everything.

For what should we thirst? It is not some finite set of "right" actions. *"Your Word is a lamp for my feet and a light on my path." (Psalm 119:105 NIV)* This means we are to follow His lead and exploit to the limit His entrepreneurial image that is at the core of our being. This doesn't occur occasionally when we happen to think of it, but daily and constantly. This is a battle of eternal life and eternal death. It does matter! To desire and pursue this is to activate the "hunger and thirst" of this Beatitude. It carries a promise that we will be filled full and satisfied. We require nothing else.

This is not the way it works in the upside down world. In the world governed by the way of the serpent, hunger and thirst are focused on very different objectives. As their own gods, humans pursue whatever is the object of immediate desire or flee to escape anything undesirable. Did you ever lie about an injury or a property loss to receive a better insurance settlement? Do you avoid your neighbor at the local market, because of a conflict or perhaps just because you don't like the person? We all do it, even those with whom God has restored His interpersonal relationship. We are all too familiar and too proficient at navigating in the upside down world. From time to time we feel guilty, because we know how readily we fall back into the way of the serpent. What makes us different is God's grace. It enables us to heed the call to return to the relationship with God. Martin Luther expressed it very well when he admonished us to return to and renew our baptismal vows and daily "drown" Satan with the promise in the water and Word of God (Luther, Martin. The Large Catechism. Translated by F. Bente and W.H.T. Dau. St. Louis, Concordia Publishing House, 1921. pp.565-773).

In the midst of pursuing God's righteousness there is no place for animosity, deceit, lies, slander, violence, or other rebellious acts against God or our fellow man. God is our Father. We are His children and heirs. Jesus knew this. He trusted His Son-ship and held tightly to the promises of the Father. He lost everything, except this: He knew He was the Son and fulfilled the Father's purpose, even to death. Here is our righteousness and victory, for it is a battle to the death. Jesus defeats the upside down world of the serpent, Satan, and death itself for US.

It is all ours, simply because God wants us to be His friends. It is not a handout, however, but a call to entrepreneurial action. To remain on the sidelines is to bury our talent and complain that we have not been equipped as well as others. Neither should we try to copy the success path that others have taken. Your talent is unique. No one else has received the image of God in the exact way as you have. Look for opportunities to exploit your talent to praise God and to serve others.

Blessed are the merciful, for they shall obtain mercy.

The way of the serpent reduces life to a subsistence level and only the strong survive. People are pitted against everything and everyone. It is a world ruled by the tree of the knowledge of good and evil and we are woefully ill-equipped. It isn't so much mankind's arrogance that the serpent exploits as human naiveté and insecurity, though a fragile and gullible ego does make it easier. Humanity is in over its head. The only strategy that comes to mind is to employ the vestige of God's image, unearned and undeserved, to enter a battle that cannot be won. The serpent sees it and laughs, for the simpletons don't even notice they have consigned themselves to the level of living things that don't possess the gift of God's image. Then they misuse that very gift to abuse the earth and subjugate their fellow-humans, often in violent fashion.

Humans, however, weary of endless struggle. Their mutual inability to destroy each other leads to a truce of sorts, though not a solution, for that would require reconciliation with the Creator and mankind doesn't have the will or power. The accommodation is called the moral law. Even that was placed in human hearts by God, yet another gift. It is conscience, central to law and order in human society since earliest times. It is manifest as government and appears in many forms: the Ten Commandments, the Code of Hammurabi, Confucianism, and the Magna Carta, to name a few.

People cannot attain their goal of domination so they turn to justice, adjudicated by a supposed "neutral" party. Justice is hailed as a great virtue. Administering it is another matter and betrays human duplicity at every turn, for there is no disinterested third party. If a biased outcome can be guaranteed, the lust and fear of the tree of knowledge of good and evil are still frustrated. Before long, it becomes necessary for justice to move to its next level. It evolves into equality, which mutates to equality of outcome. It doesn't seem fair that some excel while others fail, some are rich and others are poor, some excel in school as others drop out, some are talented athletes and others can't walk and chew gum at the same time. Justice is made to be the ally of selfishness, promising to make sure everyone is equal in all matters. When we destroy the notion of God's gifts, then joy and thanksgiving are also trashed. For what is there to be thankful? The way of the serpent is hopeless. Intent never changes. The unquenchable thirst of mankind is to control others. A human as his or her own god is the epitome of naiveté and insecurity – and appalling cruelty.

Do you want justice and rights? Do you really want what you earn and deserve? A picture of judgment day is portrayed by Jesus in a parable about sheep and goats. The sheep are praised for ministering to Jesus with food, drink, clothes, and comfort. Jesus welcomes them to the Father's eternal kingdom. The goats are condemned for their failure to do so. Both protest that they never saw Jesus in need. The goats even add that if they had, they would certainly have responded generously. Both are judged on the basis of their actions toward others: *"...for as much as you did it..."* or *"...did not do so unto Me." (Matthew 25:31-46 NIV)* The lesson is that the judgment scenario is not based on merit. Is "fair" what you seek? Are you sure? If so, you're a fool. If that is how you stand before your Maker and Judge, you may not be pleased with the outcome.

Jesus comes into this upside down world and turns it on its head. He rejects outright the notion that the hope of mankind is embodied in justice and rights. He reveals God's entrepreneurial alternative: *"Be merciful, just as your Father is merciful. Do not judge, and you will not be judged. Do not condemn, and you will not be condemned. Forgive and you will be forgiven." Luke 6:36-37 NIV)* Jesus not only says this, it is also what He does.

Perhaps the most amazing thing in His entrepreneurial response to the upside down world is that He came at all. If God was concerned with justice and rights He would have destroyed the whole mess when the serpent first convinced man and woman they could be gods. That, however, is not God's way: not justice and rights, but pity and mercy and the miracle of His Son. God stayed His course. Only God would think of such a response. Do you seek upside down or right side up?

Our response is to be no less entrepreneurial. Yet, when we follow Jesus' lead we will not be popular. The serpent loathes anything and anyone that shows his upside down-ness for what it is. It gets nasty and maybe worse, much worse. So, what are you prepared to do – entrepreneurially? Demanding justice and rights is not the answer. Rather, it is to receive the evil like Job: *"Shall we accept good from God, and not trouble?" (Job 2:10 NIV)* Ouch! This will likely leave a scar. No one said this will be easy or painless. Our entrepreneurial faith and action are to mirror the life of Jesus. He didn't demand rights, but simply received what was given, even when it is what neither He, nor we, would desire to receive.

In heaven, there is no justice; only mercy. This is God's entrepreneurial strategy and action. It is to be emulated by us.

Blessed are the pure in heart, for they shall see God.

In His Image

Human intellect and knowledge are impressive. One of the notable components of God's image is the rational mind with its power of abstract thinking. But why is it that, even with keen minds, we just can't see God? The answer is found, once again, in the garden: the ego and arrogance that got the man and woman into trouble in the first place. Humans imagine they can be objective and think dispassionately about themselves, the world, and about God. It is the serpent's lie, yet again. One can be objective only if there is no vested interest – and we are anything but neutral. It is not possible to be disinterested. We parade our "objective" findings before anyone who will listen. "Brilliant", says mankind to itself. As our own god we answer only to ourselves. Our very will demands that we see what we want to see. Who needs God? Everything is fine.

Since the gift of God's image cannot be denied or discredited, the way of the serpent must distort it: not just a little, but tortured and twisted until it ends up in an "upside down" posture. I have a memory from 1965-66 when I was in graduate school. It was a time of free speech and protests against war. It was also the time of the neo-intellectual deduction that "God is dead". Nietzsche philosophized about the death of God in the early 1880s, but it did not become a popular U.S. theological movement until the mid-1960s (Nietzsche, Friedrich. The Gay Science. 1882, Translated by Kaufmann, Walter. Vintage Books, 1974. ISBN 0-39471985-9, Section 125).

God is dead. Imagine that! What man can dream of, he can do. Most accept this axiom at face value. So, why not kill God? It takes care of the troublesome notions about right and wrong, conscience, integrity, honesty, and everything else represented by the way of the Lord. Truth is the main casualty. Man has contorted and manipulated the concept of truth to the point that many conclude it is only a relative term. This is not trivial, for it allows the serpent to focus on any issue without worrying about truth as a constant. And, once God has been killed, the lord of evil is killed just as easily. The serpent is delighted, for if he can secret himself he can move about and do his deeds freely. There is one truth, however, and it is the way of the Lord. Mankind, of its own strength and will, cannot embrace it. Any other pathway, literally, is the way of the serpent. The serpent doesn't care which course is chosen. Except for truth, they are all his.

In the midst of earth's chaos, purposefully orchestrated by the serpent, the right side up Jesus enters. He just messes up the whole thing. The serpent knows he is no match, yet he never gives up. He can't. It is his special curse. In desperation, he tries a frontal attack. After forty days of fasting in the desert, Jesus is hungry and His resistance is low. Satan is full of suggestions and ideas like turning stones into bread and putting Himself in harm's way to see if God will really protect him. Finally, the devil promises earthly power and riches if Jesus will simply focus on Himself instead of His Father. It is the same ploy used in the Garden. We may look at this story and think it is silly to even imagine Jesus falling for Satan's temptations. After all, He's really God and would never do such a thing. We forget that Jesus was in the same condition as the first humans in the Garden. He was just as susceptible to the serpent as they. Adam and Eve had the same choice to rebuke temptation. So do we in our restored bond with the Creator.

Jesus is true to the Father and to His promises. The serpent takes a drastic strategy: kill Jesus. With Jesus gone, the serpent wins and the world can relax and follow the way of the serpent without having to ever "see" God. A diabolical (how apt) plot is

113

hatched and the serpent finds an accomplice in one of Jesus' disciples. Perhaps Judas was convinced his betrayal would force Jesus' hand and the coming of God's kingdom would be hastened. How about the serpent's other partner in crime? It is the church, God forbid! The church of Jesus' day wanted proof, a sign that would validate His credentials. How ironic. They would have to kill Jesus to get their sign. The serpent is clever, indeed. Does the church of today bear the same guilt?

"Blessed are the pure in heart" is Jesus answer. A pure heart sees God without signs. A heart that is not pure cannot see God. Lepers, tax collectors, harlots, the sick, those who knew they were outside of God's kingdom found forgiveness and healing in Jesus. Their hearts were purified by God's forgiveness in Jesus' life and death. Eternal life, unearned, is given as the inheritance for all believers. Purification of a heart is painful. It requires death. Remember the planted seed? It has to rot before new life emerges. The previous self, the one who follows the way of the serpent, must be destroyed. That self is raised as a new self and returned solely by God's gift and action to the relationship that existed in the beginning. This is entrepreneurial behavior by God and His Son. It is also our entrepreneurial response and behavior that sees God and does the same.

Blessed are the peacemakers, for they shall be called the sons of God.

Followers of the way of the serpent joke derisively that anyone who believes such gibberish must live in some alternate universe. Most of the time, peace is associated with the power to kill. As a child I liked western movies. The peace officer, or sheriff, always carried a gun and kept the bad guys at bay. In world events, peacekeeping is a function of the United Nations. Troops

114

are armed with the latest weapons. Message: if you don't behave you may be arrested and if you resist you may be killed. Some peace!

Battles and wars are not limited to rival armies. The most common and devastating are waged among and between individuals: spouses, families, neighbors, rival schools, and gangs. There is no end. It seems there is no peace without conflict. Chinese philosophy calls it yin and yang and holds that it is not possible to have peace without war.

Mankind has tried war and doesn't like it. Mind you, it's not so terrible if victory can be assured. Yet, the costs are astronomical, especially in terms of lost and shattered lives. Surely, adults can attain peace among themselves. Wise and mature people should be able to resolve differences. Nations agree to stop fighting, at least for the time being, and a great fuss is made that the rivals are beating their swords into plowshares. In the 60's, people, especially the young, wrote poetry and songs about the lion and lamb lying down together absent conflict. One wonders how many realize that these analogies are from the Bible. People endure cease-fire agreements, truces, the Cold War, disarmament negotiations, and the SALT Treaties. More distressing are the constant and ever-increasing taxes to maintain armies and armaments.

At a personal level, peace is equally elusive and tenuous. It is administered by a parent, teacher, boss, peace officer, military superior, or other authoritative figures. In most societies, peace is administered by police, courts, judges, and prisons. More than 1,250,000 lawyers in America are paid to help others adjudicate and resolve differences.

115

In His Image

In our upside down world, peace consists of terms dictated by the strongest party. This is peace that results from the sheer capacity to dominate and overwhelm a given situation. In past times, some not so far back, a father dominated his wife and children without objection or question, a teacher's word was law, and bosses had total control of the lives they supervised. At the country level, soldiers of a victorious army looted conquered territory and raped all females in reach. The U.S. broke precedent after the surrender of Germany and Japan by returning captured land and possessions (except for military hardware) and assisting the conquered in rebuilding government and industrial infrastructures. Prior to that, victorious armies often annexed enemy land and at times enslaved the populace. Today's U.N. tries to keep peace, but with mixed results. The best that can be done by the upside down world is to manufacture peace by force. That is not peace.

Jesus inverted it. He discredited the peace of the conqueror. He rejected the kingship offered by the serpent. He refused to accommodate "church" leaders who offered to declare Him king if He would show a sign that met their demands. Had He taken this path, He could have achieved their kind of peace, but it would have been the way of the serpent. Or, He could have given them the sign of Judgment Day, with God's wrath and damnation. He did neither. Instead, He kept His focus on the battle for human hearts and the demand for complete surrender to the Father.

"Shock and Awe" is the only way to describe Jesus' entrepreneurial behavior. It defines His role as Peacemaker. Why did God choose this path? It would have been much easier to create peace by destroying the whole notion and mess of humans in His image and creating perfectly obedient robots. He didn't. The full purpose of God in creation was to have a son, created in His image. He wanted a son with whom He could enjoy a relationship of mutual love, trust, and openness, a son who would create as the Father creates. God didn't make a mistake. There was no need to destroy His handiwork. Even Christians sometimes misunderstand this.

God's entrepreneurial behavior as a peacemaker employs a dual strategy. First, Jesus is the perfect Son. He is no hoax. Jesus did not keep His divine nature and come to earth in disguise. He was human. He set aside His divine nature so He might be human in every way as at creation. He stared down and exposed the serpent's lies, trusting the Word and Promise of the Creator. It really galls the serpent when his lies are exposed and he has no place to hide.

Second, Jesus allowed mankind to have its way. Though mankind is the marionette and Satan is the puppeteer, mankind is no less guilty. The serpent was sure that his strategy and tactics would prove victorious and permanently rid him of the Son. What a wicked irony of ironies, the very thing the devil did to the perfect and obedient Son was Satan's own undoing. He is "hoist by his own petard." You see, Jesus' victory – and ours – is not realized in upside down power, but in right side up obedience chosen freely, not by force.

It was the last Adam who lived the life the first Adam was intended to live. He is the Son who never lusts and fears under the yoke of the tree of the knowledge of good and evil. It is the Son who always and only serves the Father and his fellowmen. The Son does not have to think or be concerned about His own welfare, for he is in the hands and under the protection of the Father. His divine nature is resumed and He inherits the Kingdom. It was His even in His time of human nature, because that is what the Father promised.

Has the world ever been in greater need of peacemakers? We have the same name, promise, and calling as the last Adam. For what are we waiting?

Blessed are those who are persecuted for righteousness' sake, for theirs is the kingdom of heaven.
Blessed are you when men revile you and persecute you and utter all kinds of evil against you falsely on my account. Rejoice and be glad, for your reward is great in heaven, for so men persecuted the prophets who were before you.

Persecution is on the rise. Annually, over 100,000 die for their Christian faith and the number is increasing. We shouldn't be taken aback, however, for the serpent abhors truth and constantly searches for ways to blunt its power. One way is to intimidate the opposition or, when possible, even eliminate it.

Persecution is something we avoid by nature. No one wants to suffer. Rarely, a believer may be required to declare faith and accept the consequences, but generally it does not come to such a stark choice. It is easy to stay quiet when controversial topics arise. The simplest way to avoid persecution is conformity to socially acceptable behavior. Yet, conformity can raise the stakes on one's faith without warning. St. Paul counsels: *"Do not conform any longer to the pattern of this world, but be transformed by the renewing of your mind. Then you will be able to test and approve what God's will is – His good, pleasing and perfect will." (Romans 12:2 NIV)*

Political correctness is a case in point. Target groups must be careful of what they say, write, and even think. Don't use words denounced as offensive, insensitive, racist, sexist, or homophobic. The term started as a joke, though its humor is dark. In the U.S.S.R. it was understood that using "inappropriate" words, regardless of actions, might determine the outcome of political situations, often with life and death consequences. Political correctness, in fact, is viewed by many to be analogous to cultural Marxism. It echoes much of George Orwell's thought in <u>Animal Farm</u>. Totalitarian rule is about the power of people over other people. It has been aptly labeled as man's inhumanity to man. If you have the power, simply lie and liquidate without consequences. The serpent always has his way with those who would be gods.

Politicians are often the most adept. They rely on "low-information" voters who believe they will benefit personally in exchange for support. It is helpful if the leader has the active backing of the media. A negative event is easily minimized if it is not reported, to the point that no one is held responsible. The opposite can also be true when false information is presented as fact. The world is big and there are so many incidents that, unless news reporters exercise integrity, ordinary people may be uninformed, under-informed, or misinformed. The situation has improved with Internet access. Yet, the caution still applies: "Believe none of what you read and only half of what you see" (Though some attribute this quote to Mark Twain, Benjamin Franklin receives credit at http://www.dictionary-quotes.com).

The root of the problem is that the serpent manipulates human reasoning. This is wickedly ironic, since it involves use of a part of the image of God, given to each of us. Unless we believe and have faith in God's Word, we cannot know truth with certainty

119

and perceive it from the evidence we have. The serpent twists the truth and creates false perceptions by manipulating the facts. It is appalling how the establishment of what is politically correct is used to present falsehood as reality and truth. Besides discerning this behavior in political leaders, it is also an ingredient in advertising. Closer to home, it is a common ploy used in interpersonal relationships.

While conformity is a key tactic of political correctness, it is a weapon used by the serpent in many other battles as well. Conformity, however, is not the issue. It is merely the symptom of what motivates and dictates a person's allegiance. We serve either God or ourselves. This is what Jesus refers to when He tells us to deny ourselves. Our commitment must be to the relationship the Creator established by giving us His name, His promise, and the calling to which each of us is to be dedicated. After humans denied God to follow the way of the serpent, our bond with Him was restored by the life and death of His Son. Once again, we are free to follow His directive to subdue and have dominion over the earth by serving God and our fellowmen. Our sole purpose is to create in the mode and name of the Creator. We become and remain right side up through His power, while the serpent through his minions is always working to re-invert us. You may see no reason to resist. It seems everyone does it. Why not conform when it is all we see or hear?

There are groups that do not conform at all and put it in the face of society. For whatever reason, they are not accepted or do not wish to conform to ground rules, and choose disruption as their primary action. The rebellion is sometimes violent, as in the case of gangs. Yet, even in these groups conformity is demanded, with penalties for breaking the code of behavior that can be most severe, including death.

To subdue and have dominion over God's creation is a call to be heroic, without heroes, daring to live entrepreneurial lives unafraid as sons and daughters of the King. We are also to rectify the damage inflicted by the way of the serpent. This the upside down world loathes. It loves and has pride in itself only. Mankind cannot see the self-destruction it causes. Above all, it will not confess its hopelessness and lost-ness. It cannot live in the way of the Lord, because that would require acknowledgment of a superior intellect and power. Yet, humans cannot see that they live under the thumb of the serpent, much more powerful and clever than we mortals. Mankind argues that the upside down world might have a few glitches, but basically it is in good shape, ready for the next big human advancement. A little religion can even be helpful if it doesn't mess with the system.

This is a buzz saw for even the most prepared. To enter it in the humility of the Beatitudes seems suicidal. We are maligned for racism, homophobia, and pro-choice transgressions when we don't parrot politically correct talking points. Our faith-based lives are minimalized and ridiculed as out of touch and archaic dodges to the "real" issues of the day. Why not steer clear and let the upside down world reap its just reward? We've addressed this point more than once. Standing idly by is self-centered and upside down. Our call is to serve God and our fellowman. The Spirit guides us and helps us to remember our posture before God is always the same. We are guilty, but forgiven. This is our confidence and assurance against all evidence to the contrary, that our interpersonal relationship with the Creator is held intact by Him. From it spring the intentional motivation and attitude that pursue the same kinds of relationships with others.

It is the essence of the parable about the Samaritan who found the wounded person at the side of the road, as well as those about the lost sheep, the lost coin, and the prodigal son. The Creator's response is not the fire and brimstone that might be our inclination, but mercy and grace that condemn sin, not the sinner. To us sinners He offers an alternate plan, which models God's entrepreneurial behavior in Jesus and returns us to the original relationship. God sticks with His original plan, the right plan. Like the servants with five and two talents, we are to be in the service of the Master and our fellow men. One qualifying note: service to our fellowmen is not limited to those who follow the right side up way of the Lord, but to those living the upside down way of the serpent as well. Don't expect it to be easy, but know that the image of God in you is stronger than all the forces of the way of the serpent. We needn't fret for ourselves. Our name, our promise, and our calling are intact, guarded by the Creator Giver.

After His triumphal ride into Jerusalem, Jesus sought fruit from a fig tree. When there was none He cursed the tree. The following day the disciples saw the withered tree and remembered with some awe the incident of the previous evening. Some commentators see a strong relationship between the dead tree and the church of Jesus' day. How about the church today? Is the church producing the fruit demanded by a perfect God? The invisible church is not dead, because it is made up of all believers, whom Father, Son, and Spirit see and know. So, why is the visible church in a state of continuing decline? The church is supposed to be like the inn in the parable, to which the injured traveler was taken. The inn accommodates and provides shelter for the wounded person and the Samaritan, but it controls neither. The church dare not try to build a "box" and put God inside it, thinking it can define God or His children. Let God be God. Actually, He is. We fool only ourselves when we fall into the way of the serpent by thinking or acting otherwise.

God wants heroic sons and daughters who trust the Father enough to let go of everything else. This is heroism without heroes. There are no victory parades or medals. These people act out of what they are, not because of what they may receive. Let go of the things of this world, so that you may receive the inheritance of earth and heaven: dignity, joy, security, ambition, justice, wisdom, and peace. These are blessings promised in the Beatitudes.

Chapter 7

Discussion Questions

1. The author uses Jesus' Parable of the Talents to explain God's grace and the variety of human responses. How do you see the truths of the parable demonstrated in today's world and in your life?

2. How do we attempt to dominate God and other people instead of loving God and others?

3. What does it mean to "hunger and thirst for righteousness"?

4. How can mercy and an entrepreneurial spirit coexist?

5. How do the beatitudes inform and empower your entrepreneurial life?

Chapter Eight

Image of God

As we explore the power of entrepreneurial behavior, the potential to re-energize American free enterprise becomes evident. American exceptionalism is not a reach, but merely a display of the individual creativity and initiative that resides in every person. Mankind is already exceptional, but it is not the doing of any man or woman. It is beyond the reach of the tree of the knowledge of good and evil. It surpasses the way of the serpent. Human exceptionalism is God's doing. It occurred at creation when mankind received divine DNA in the image of God. This is surely a foundation from which to rediscover our freedom and revitalize free enterprise. Yet, there must be more to our horizon than merely a return to economic and political success. Our purpose is greater than nationalism, as patriotically appealing as that may seem. We are called to be God's partners in His own prosperity, *"...where moth and rust do not destroy, and where thieves do not break in and steal." (Matthew 6:20 NIV)* He has commissioned us to subdue and have dominion over creation. It isn't complicated or spectacular. It doesn't require special training or equipment. There is no secret set of rules or special handshake to be one with whom He seeks to have such a truly awesome interpersonal relationship.

The image of God has been received by every human. It affords unlimited access to a storehouse of resources and assures success. Endowed with His image, we have been given an immortal soul of inestimable worth. We are enabled to distinguish right from wrong, contemplate the abstract, and communicate with Him and each other. In the capacity to create we mirror His use of

125

knowledge, understanding, and wisdom. These are rendered complete by His entrepreneurial gifts of faith and action. We have more than we need to carry out His charge: *"My grace is sufficient for you." (2 Corinthians 12:9 NIV)*

Besides Scripture, the work of three writers was used to develop "Image of God" materials: Richard Deem (www.godandscience.org/contact.html) "The Human Difference: How Humans are Unique Compared to *All* Other Animals"; Peter May (www.bethinking.org/resources/what-is-the-image-of-god.htm) "What is the Image of God?"; J. Rendle-Short (1981) "Man: The Image of God."

The creation of man and woman in God's image and its meaning do not occur in a vacuum. The story begins with a chaotic, formless earth and universe (all universes). He shapes everything, positions earth in the universe, and then fills it with many life forms. Prior to creating humans, however, the Creator seems to pay no special attention to specific objects in the creative process. He says, "Let there be" and it is so. This is not to say that creation isn't a momentous display of omnipotence. We can't even contemplate such power much less rival it.

Then God focuses attention on the crown of His creation. *"Let us make man in our image."* He is actively involved and forms the human from dirt and blows the "breath of life" into the nostrils. God's action bestows divine DNA, though not the entire inventory. In comparison with God's attributes of omnipotence, omniscience, and omnipresence, humanity isn't even close. The image of God, however, is a significant presence. The Creator shares His entrepreneurial character traits so that we have everything we need to fulfill His directive to subdue and have dominion over His creation. An exhaustive catalog of the blessings of His image is not possible, nor is it the point. Examples included here are intended to facilitate a better understanding of the use God wants us to make of His gifts.

Divine Character Traits

Value: Creation of mammals occurs toward the end of the Genesis narrative. They survive by what they hear, see, smell, taste, and touch along with instinctive impulses and urges. They live to pursue what is desired and avoid what is feared. Then they die and that is their end.

Human DNA is a close anatomical and physiological match with the chimpanzee. God, however, endowed humans with components of His image, rendering irreconcilable differences between humans and every other creature, poles apart. Value is a significant element of that image. First, He names humans His children, the same designation as Jesus, our brother. *"You are my Son, whom I love; with you I am well pleased." (Mark 1:11 NIV).* Second, the name carries a promise that we will inherit God's earth and heaven. *"Now if we are children, then we are heirs – heirs of God and co-heirs with Christ" (Romans 8:17 NIV).* Third, God forms a bond and partnership with those He names, to jointly carry out His temporal and eternal mission: *"for it is God who works in you to will and to act according to His good purpose. (Philippians 2:13 NIV)* This is truly exceptional! What more could we ever need or ask?

Truth & Freedom: There were more casualties than just the mortality of humans when the serpent seduced them with the lie that they could be their own gods. It was the ultimate "either/or", aptly described by Whittaker Chambers as well as numerous

127

theologians. Their fateful decision marked the end of innocence and, as warned by the Creator, it condemned them to death. Opting for a foolish and false power grab, the precepts of truth and freedom were lost, precisely what the humans thought their behavior would unlock. To their chagrin and mortification, these tenets could not then or today be duplicated, replaced, or redefined, regardless of the most diligent, though selfish intents and endeavors. They were outwitted by the serpent, beguiled into using the very image received from the Creator to declare God as unnecessary and extraneous. Humans disdainfully determined they were the highest authority. In reality, mankind is a distant third out of three.

Regarding truth, humanity seeks its own, grasping for anything that gratifies the lust of desire and rejecting whatever stokes fear. Pilate famously confronted Jesus with a philosophical and rhetorical question: "Quid Est Veritas?" What is truth? We reveal our inconsequential smallness every time we assume we possess the highest form of reasoning and conclude that if mankind has no answer then there must be no answer. It must be comical to God, but for its seriousness. It is deadly serious.

The self-centered way of the serpent leads us to warp the definition of truth in order to empower desire and reject fear. If we are the highest form of intelligence, then it is impossible for our truth to not be so. Yet, this does not hold up to the light of experience, especially when another person is stronger. This self-contradiction is inescapable unless we are released from our self-centered existence. God is truth, but is a nonentity in the realm of human gods.

Mankind arbitrarily deems it feasible to remove God from reality, thereby denying truth itself. Religion is not scrapped, for at times it is useful. The serpent uses it against intransigents, to manipulate them into thinking God is accessible to those clever and strong enough to exhibit self-worth. The serpent doesn't care which road is taken, so long as it is not the way of the Lord. We are easily conned to conclude that, when we suppose we create our own life and destiny, we are not serving the god of mammon. God or Satan: each of us serves one or the other. We are blind and fail to recognize that in serving ourselves, we serve Satan, the ultimate deceiver. We have placed ourselves under the tree of the knowledge of good and evil, the law of nature by which the rest of the creation was meant to be ruled. Then, we die: and, for what? The price and prize is eternal separation from God.

As to freedom, the second precept, it figures prominently in mankind's creation and life. The crown of God's creation was a responsible creature with a mind that empowered freedom and action. On the other hand, animals were created with five senses and instinctive capacity. They dominate weakness and flee strength. There is no rational thought or free will. Freedom makes humans unsuitable denizens in dictatorial settings, even after the failure in the garden. The crash of the first Adam meant the collapse of freedom in terms of obedience to God. Once un-done, it could not be re-done. Without freedom, each person is his or her own god whose only purpose is to serve self. This also is life under the tree of the knowledge of good and evil. It is a contradiction of God's image.

We humans are so easily fooled and captivated. The serpent cleverly begins with God's gifts and entices us to expand and distort them. It leads to poor decisions with unintended and unwanted consequences. The serpent presented a false choice that mankind could, by the simple act of free will, rid itself of authority. Too late, it became clear that what they accomplished was an unequal trade-off of a loving Father for a cruel tormenter. They distorted liberty as an excuse to exercise freedom as if it had no consequences. That is not freedom, but the way of the serpent. We either serve the way of the Lord or the way of the serpent. The effort to remove God from human life is endless. Satan's great lie is that, if God can be eliminated, we are free to do as we please. Yet, the way of the serpent is itself a belief system. The Lord's way seems rigid and unreasonable, while the serpent's way is presented as logical and laid-back. It is apparent that attempting to analyze God only entrenches us deeper in the way of the serpent.

Humans still seek freedom, but usually in the wrong places and the wrong way. Consider the new nations in the world seeking freedom from various forms of tyranny. Too often, the only change is one tyrant for another. America's free speech movement in the mid-1960s is another example. At the time, I was attending graduate school at the University of California. Though it is illogical that freedom has anything to do with random shouting of four letter words through a megaphone, the way of the serpent prevailed. Then it was determined that drugs would lead to freedom – or civil liberties, removal of censorship, disbanding marriage, or the right to abort the unborn, even post-birth. Killing does not cease to be murder by changing the definition. Under the sway of the serpent, freedom always mutates into imprisonment that manifests itself in many and various unintended consequences.

Mankind was utterly lost with no hope for regaining freedom. Yet, at the time of His calculation, God created the reality of the last Adam and brought freedom back. Now, shielded by the perfect obedience of the True Son, we receive a full pass by our Father and Judge. We are complicit in sin, but contribute nothing to its solution, except the damning act of the former that necessitated the redeeming act of the latter. It is God's play – His choice and action alone.

By faith, freedom is re-gifted. It re-establishes the relationship between God and mankind and seals it. To us this is nonsense. In his explanation of the Second Article in the Apostles' Creed, Luther says: "I believe that I cannot, by my own reason or strength, believe in Jesus Christ my Lord or come to him." Remove the parenthetical phrase: "I believe that I cannot...believe..." It is not logical to us, but for God it computes perfectly. That's why He's God and we're not. The only way it can be negated is if we return to the pride that insists we can manage it ourselves or reject it as unimportant.

While humans are not the serpent's equal, neither is the serpent any match for the Creator. The serpent felt certain God was cornered by His own pronouncement of death for disobedience. God is not the serpent's fool. Satan was defeated and left twisting in the wind when God sent His Son to live the life intended of Adam and then to die to pay the price of God's justice. Humanity was not destroyed for its capitulation, though it was the prescribed penalty. For whatever reason, He sent a substitute to suffer the consequences on our behalf. That is God's desire and will. It shows how much He values His own creation.

We live in a fallen world, yet He lives among us, in this broken realm. He has brought us back to the original bond with the Creator. The faith He implants enables us to reject the self-centered life the serpent would have us follow. With faith we receive freedom, but not the autonomous self-directed life and action that marks of the way of the serpent. It is freedom in the image of God. In his 1520 treatise, "On Christian Freedom," Luther pronounced with classic simplicity: "A Christian man is the most free lord of all, and subject to none; a Christian man is the most dutiful servant of all, and subject to every one." The serpent's self-centered presuppositions render this statement not only dichotomous, but entirely meaningless. Luther was, however, merely restating the answer Jesus gave to the lawyer: serve God and fellowman. This is the directive to subdue and have dominion over His creation. It is the great commission, to share the Good News that the path back to our Creator awaits us. Don't reject it. Don't miss out, for your eternity depends on it.

We cannot know the mind of God. His actions are often bewildering. All we can rationalize is that a plan requiring the death of God's own Son must be truly momentous. The upshot is that we are as important to God as His Own Son. How else can the Son's life and death be explained? It is what He tells us: *"You are my Son; today I have become your Father." (Psalm 2:7 NIV)*. This bestows incalculable worth on us, though we have no part in the action or merit. It is humbling, as it should be.

When we contemplate our own personal value and worth, we inevitably fall into the serpent's trap of self-centeredness, yet again. Don't think about it, just live it! When our son was very young, he enjoyed music and danced, uninhibited. Our response to God for giving us value of such magnitude should be spontaneous, like a child. Jesus used this example to emphasize faith and action when His disciples argued about their importance. He must have been exasperated by their self-centeredness. *"...I tell you the truth, unless you change and become like little children, you will never*

132

enter the kingdom of heaven. Therefore whoever humbles himself like this child is the greatest in the kingdom of heaven." (Matthew 18:3-4 NIV)

Freedom doesn't give us license to act randomly. Rather, it is the basis of entrepreneurial motive and attitude. Motive is what inspires us. Attitude is our mindset. Both are driven by the Spirit of God and predispose us to a purpose and point of view in life, the inspiration and outlook that drive creativity and initiative.

This creative and intentional drive impelled Abraham to leave family and homeland, become a pilgrim, and follow the directive of a "new" God. It is the same Spirit that led our ancestors to a new country. Entrepreneurial DNA is the Spirit of inventiveness and work ethic in a free market. It facilitates the pursuit of happiness guaranteed in the Declaration of Independence. Socialism, communism, and fascism don't work, for they subjugate people and seek to crush the Spirit of freedom. An entitlement mentality robs people of freedom to serve God and others. Our restored freedom is not served by handouts from God or government. Entitlement is self-centeredness at its worst. It destroys thanksgiving and joy. Instead, we are to use our freedom to produce all we can with all the talents bestowed on us. It is the same risk, thought, creativity, and energy that is modeled for us by the Creator Himself.

When God is denied, the foundation of freedom is negated. Cardinal Joseph Ratzinger, Pope Benedict XVI, published an article in the Spring 1996 issue of COMMUNIO titled, *Truth and Freedom.* He strikes at the heart of the matter in his conclusion. "If there is no truth about man, man also has no freedom."

The Son tells us: *"...you will know the truth, and the truth will set you free." (John 8:32 NIV)* Truth and freedom are restored.

Immortality: It is difficult to fathom perpetual existence. We are bound by the dimension of time. God is not, but was present, omnipresent in fact, before the beginning. He has always been, is, and always will be. Under the tree of the knowledge of good and evil and the serpent's misguided model of humans as gods, "survival of the fittest" becomes the essence of their feeble attempt to explain how everything evolved and has come to be. Anything not visible and tangible is treated at best with doubt, more likely denial. Yet, living organisms cling to life at all costs, at times adapting to the most challenging conditions, in order to secure food and avoid extinction. There is an innate drive for self-preservation and self-perpetuation. The instinct to breed and propagate manifests itself in whole species as well as individuals. Mankind seeks, but has not found an incontrovertible answer for the dynamic that drives plants, animals, and humans to achieve perpetual continuance. In our state of alienation from God, the urge for immortality can take on strange trappings. In times past, it was considered almost normal for kings and others to dispose of a wife, merely because she didn't produce a male heir. It dented man's pride to learn the male species carries the gender gene. Graveyards are filled with symbols, monuments, and obelisks, of this desire to be immortal.

God has no beginning and no end. He simply IS! Though all of us will die, we each have an immortal soul. God intends for us, after time on earth, to spend eternity in heaven, where a sinless nature is sealed forever. He also tells us about the alternative. Mankind doesn't like it, so the glib solution is to declare that "God is dead" and hell does not exist. Yet, there is a niggling suspicion that when we die perhaps we don't go to nothingness, like a swatted mosquito. Just what is your description of a permanent condition in which God has entirely removed His presence, if not hell? What is your immortal intention and destination? Earthly life is temporal. God's children, redeemed by Christ, will live with Him forever. Those who reject Him will be separated from God, also forever. Will they lose His image and its benefits? For sure this is an unknown, but what if the sole remaining piece of God's image is immortality: endless suffering and horror that recognizes the significance of what has been lost, along with the ultimate and utter falseness, emptiness, and stupidity of the way of the serpent.

Perfection: To err is not human, as stated in a popular axiom. In their original created state, humans were sinless: innately moral, ethical, just, honest, honorable, and principled. Although they were not omniscient, humans did everything perfectly and without arrogance. The Creator interacted with them on a regular basis. Perhaps, God shared a type of telepathic communication with them. His interpersonal relationship with humans was based on equality between the parties, though this might be a bit difficult to comprehend. When man and woman succumbed to the serpent's lure, their sinless states ceased immediately.

Yet, a significant vestige remains. Humans still seek to be virtuous. We recognize, and at times aspire to, the values of honesty, morality, and justice. That is, so long as it doesn't interfere with other intents and motives. We still seek beauty and holiness, but no longer through a simple faith relationship that recognizes and accepts creation as pure gift for which we can only give thanks. We are self-contaminated. In an entitlement frame of mind, thankfulness and joy are replaced with greed and pride. Instead of dominion over the earth as God directed, people seek to

135

gain control over others. Mankind is bent (hell-bent?) on being its own god and dominating others.

Relational: To have an interpersonal relationship with God is, in fact, the reason we were given the image of our Creator. Perhaps, it is the reason for creation itself. Wrap your mind around that! God wants a relationship with each of us. His is a loving nature, expressed by an interpersonal relationship with each of us. When humans opted to follow the way of the serpent, God sent His Son, not to administer justice, but to rebuild the path back to the relationship God desired from eternity. The perfect life of Christ links us back to that relationship with all the interactions and attributes we have come to understand about friends. Jesus even uses that term while talking to His disciples: *"You are my friends...I have called you friends, for everything that I learned from My Father I have made known to you...This is my command: Love each other." (John 15:14-17 NIV)* It is the way friends treat each other. Not so amazingly, relationships have two essential characteristics: faith and action, the two traits of entrepreneurs.

This work is not difficult to know and understand. Remember, again, the answer Jesus gave the teacher of the law when asked about the most significant of God's commandments. Love God and fellow man. God's expectation is for us to create and work on interpersonal relationships. The First Table of the Law tells us about the relationship God offers and seeks with us. The Second tells us about the relationships God wants us to have with our fellow-humans, starting with one's spouse. It is no surprise that interpersonal relationships operate through the same character traits associated with entrepreneurial behavior. First, faith and trust: these form the cornerstone of relationships. Second, individual initiative: relationships function by virtue of actions between and on behalf of the parties involved. Also, it should be noted that interpersonal relationships are one-to-one associations. It is not possible to have an interpersonal relationship with a group.

Because of God's entrepreneurial action after the fall into sin, His Son came to earth and lived the life the first Adam was intended to live. God has the relationship He desires with Jesus, the "second Adam." This "last Adam" won our salvation, once and for all. Once again, God has the relationship He sought (we didn't seek it) with humans from the beginning. Jesus demonstrates how we are to fulfill the human side of this relationship. It is only as God's redeemed child that one is able to reciprocate. This is done by "putting on Christ" and returning to the original condition. "Putting on Christ" happens in baptism and it is this state for which every Christian strives. It is also the model for interpersonal relationships with our fellow-humans.

Intelligent: We each have a rational mind that allows us to analyze and reach conclusions in all areas of life. Our intelligence is grounded in the ability to speak and communicate. The Hungarian novelist, Arthur Koestler, concluded that symbolic language is the "sharpest break" between us and animals. The mind is boggling, anatomically and psychologically. Estimated storage capacity of the human brain exceeds 1,000,000,000,000,000 items of information (that is 1,000 trillion) (Koestler, A., *The Ghost in the Machine*. London. Hutchinson, 1967, p.19).

God is a communicator. This is what He and the humans did in the garden in the cool of the day. We can even imagine what they may have talked about. How did they learn to speak? Substantial scientific evidence leads one to the conclusion that spoken and written communication is innate. We can only conclude God taught them. It is one of the gifts received with the image of God. The way of the serpent works overtime to find some "acceptable" explanation, but the very best he can do is lamely declare this inborn trait is the result of "intelligent" design.

The opening of John's gospel constitutes a dissertation on God's capacity to communicate. His own Son is called the Word. It leaves no question about God's intent and action to communicate with us. What does it say about our tendency to use this gift to curse, mislead, or defraud others? An interesting and terrifying scenario emerges if we think about the capacity to communicate and whether it may be taken from those who are separated from God for eternity.

Creativity: Just as God worked in the creation of the world, we are to do the same. This is what He intends by the instruction to have dominion. God used His knowledge, understanding, and wisdom at creation. This capacity is given us to have dominion and to use the very same creative resources to constantly and continually re-create God's world and universe. It is this creative capacity that led to major advances and steps that have been taken since prehistory: the discovery of fire and its control, the invention of the wheel, irrigation, the discovery of planets orbiting the earth, and the discovery of gravity. More recently, consider the discovery of germs, cures for diseases, gravity, electricity, the atom, food preservation, motorized-transportation, air and space-travel, the Hubble telescope, and so much more. The list is endless. All this and more has come about, simply because humans have received and use God's creative resources. The way of the serpent convinces us this is of itself, a typical self-centered conclusion.

The gift of creativity remains one of wonder. We have entered the "information" age. It means that rather than creatively using matter and elements of the earth, man now creates an increasing number of intangible products from intangible components. Animals don't do this. They have no creative or abstract capacity. They reproduce identical instinctual designs time after time: spider webs, the songs of birds, migratory routes. Animals have no originality. Only humans have it.

Knowledge, Understanding, and Wisdom

Hebrews 11:3 tells us that the world was framed by the Word of God, thus manifesting the first entrepreneurial trait. Next, He made everything from things that cannot be seen, which embodies the second entrepreneurial trait. This was discussed in Chapter 2, when we reviewed the ideas of Chris Ortiz. Things that can't be seen are not necessarily nonexistent, but may only be invisible. It can be argued that, in creation, God used His perfect creativity and initiative with visible and invisible resources (that is all that exists, ever existed, and will ever exist) to create the universe in a manner that humans can comprehend. It is our work model.

Animals exist day-to-day based on senses, instincts, and urges. In their world, there is no logic or reason. At times, when animals do things together, it is described as friendship. Yet, it is not like the interpersonal relationship between two people. Though instincts come into play, like a mother hen protecting her chicks, animals can attack in an instant for food or for propagation rights. Survival of the fittest is the only rule. It dictates life and death. That's the tree of the knowledge of good and evil.

Humans are magnificently different. The Creator endowed humans with a limitless assortment of His own assets. These resources are intangible, but as real today as at creation. In His charge to subdue and have dominion over creation is an inclusive directive to discover and use them in daily life. He has commissioned us to be His partners: *"...for it is God who works in you to will and to act according to His good purpose"* *(Philippians 2:13 NIV).*

Mankind is trapped in the way of the serpent and does not recognize God's invisible resources. The way of the serpent wants us to believe these resources have come about by way of the tree of the knowledge of good and evil. We can describe an incredible array of assets at our command, but cannot explain them or identify their source. We arrogantly conclude that discoveries like the laws of gravity and physics, the law of thermodynamics, and a proliferation of technologies have come about through our own power. We smugly display the creation of an airplane, a computer, or a cell phone as a result of our own capacity to manipulate technology. Yet, mankind can only extract from the world what God created. It is a greater "leap of faith" to hold evolution's view than belief in an omnipotent, omniscient, and omnipresent God. It is ironic that God's image, bestowed on mankind at creation, is the gift that enables earthly gods to determine that it is all their doing. Who says God doesn't have a sense of humor? We know the source, yet that is not our concern. Our charge is to seek and use God's knowledge, understanding, and wisdom to continuously re-create the world in His image.

Proficiency in knowledge, understanding, and wisdom facilitates our productivity. It should not, however, be mistaken as a directive from God to abandon what we are doing to start a business. Instead, we are to live our lives as entrepreneurs, creating and working in whatever capacity we find ourselves. Creativity produces something that did not previously exist, regardless of the venue. It is accomplished every day, whatever you do and wherever you are, as an entrepreneur running a business, a conscientious entrepreneurial employee, an entrepreneurial spouse, parent, child, clerk, teacher, doctor, friend etc. You get the idea. By exercising entrepreneurial dominion in all you do, God's grace enables you to create value through which He blesses those around you. You receive value from God, not from yourself. We are simply not capable of such "God" behavior.

Each of us has received God's call to be His partner. Neither the arrogant rich fool nor the lazy servant with one talent provides our behavior model. The servants with five and two talents are the prototypical models of entrepreneurial creativeness and industriousness the Master has taught and expects.

What are we waiting for?

Chapter 8

Discussion Questions

1. Discuss the divine character traits connected with the image of God. What new insights does the dialog about these traits give you?

2. What is true freedom?

3. What are the implications of immortality for your life?

4. What does it mean to have a relationship with God?

5. The author states: "Our charge is to seek and use God's knowledge, understanding, and wisdom to re-create the world in His image." What are some practical examples of implementing this principle?

Chapter Nine

Faith and Action

Fixing Free Enterprise and Democracy

America is at an historic decision point. We can, by creative and industrious behavior, reaffirm the freedom and liberty under which the nation was founded. This path reasserts and secures the same freedom of belief, speech, association, mobility, livelihood, and wealth accumulation for all. That has been our core value since 1776. It is an uphill climb, with obstacles. Freedom takes strength and work, but it is surely what we want to restore and preserve for our children and all future generations.

The second option is the easy road of entitlements with centralized control over all aspects of our lives. It is effortless, a downhill run to totalitarianism. Cynics might say that democracy has had its chance and now it's time to try another path. The other paths have been tried. They all lead to the shackles of tyranny and oppression, without exception. We either live in freedom or we don't. In an essay written soon after World War II, Friedrich von Hayek called it "The Road to Serfdom." You should read it or re-read it. Benjamin Franklin was correct: "Those who would give up essential liberty to purchase a little temporary safety deserve neither liberty nor safety" (Benjamin Franklin, *Historical Review of Pennsylvania, 1759; US author, diplomat, inventor, physicist, politician, and printer, 1706 - 1790)*.

Some argue that, since slavery and racial prejudice were tolerated in the republic's first decades, American freedom and democracy have been discredited. Certainly, the national humiliation that was personified in the Civil War was a dark episode and a horrendous price was and is still being paid. Yet, centralized authority in the hands of elected and unelected self-styled elites leads to a more sinister bondage and cruelty. In a democracy, faults can be corrected. Abraham Lincoln nobly laid this out in his Gettysburg Address: "...this nation, under God, shall have a new birth of freedom – and...government of the people, by the people, for the people, shall not perish from the earth." The capacity to learn from and correct errors is a vital strength of democracy.

A cultural, social, or political movement is not necessary to do the right thing. Justice and rights do not occur because laws are enacted. The interests of economic prosperity aren't served by business decisions emanating from central-planning gurus. We know it! Yet, "rich fools" still dominate the economic landscape and we enable, even encourage, the servant with one talent to live a life of entitlements. Look closely. Does either caricature stare back at you from your ideological mirror?

Free enterprise and democracy cannot be fixed like a broken window or a flat tire any more than bad "karma" can be eased with a magical incantation. America's free enterprise is not owned by collective society. Socialism and communism try and re-try to use this false model. It doesn't work. America's economy consists of what each person adds to or takes from it. GDP, Gross Domestic Product, is an all-inclusive tally. Government does not add to GDP, because its entire operation is funded by taxes and other confiscations of the wealth that for-profit corporations and private individuals have generated from their own *private* capital investments.

Further, it is not possible for fairness, equality, and freedom to be dictated or legislated. Greed, fraud, and dishonesty cannot be abolished by fiat.

"...the things that come out of the mouth come from the heart, and these make a man unclean. For out of the heart come evil thoughts, murder, adultery, sexual immorality, theft, false testimony, slander." (Matthew 15:18-19 NIV)

Moral and ethical behaviors come from the heart. No earthly authority can require them. It seems we still face the same question: will it be the way of the Lord or the way of the serpent. Everyone is susceptible and must give his or her own answer.

"...there is no one on earth who is righteous, no one who does what is right and never sins. (Ecclesiastes 7:20 NIV)

The restoration of the relationship with the Creator restores entrepreneurial freedom and free will. Like Abraham, we are led by an entrepreneurial God who empowers us to trust and obey as well as emulate His own behavior.

"It is for freedom that Christ has set us free. Stand firm, then, and do not let yourselves be burdened again by a yoke of slavery" (Galatians 5:1 NIV).

This is where God dominates the entrepreneurial landscape. While humans have a vestige of the entrepreneurial image of God, it is employed for a variety of reasons, some for good purposes and others not. What sets believers apart is an entrepreneurial God. His leading sets us up with unique entrepreneurial DNA. As Christians, our motivation and attitude is not so much about free will, but a redeemed and restored will.

"...because of His great love for us, God, who is rich in mercy, made us alive with Christ even when we were dead...God raised us up with Christ and seated us with Him...in order that in the coming ages He might show the incomparable riches of His grace...For it is by grace you have been saved, through faith – and this is not from yourselves, it is the gift of God – not by works, so that no one can boast. For we are God's workmanship, created in Christ Jesus to do good works, which God prepared in advance for us to do." (Ephesians 2:4-10 NIV)

The last Adam won and has given back your freedom. Will you embrace it and abandon the easy way of the serpent? Or, will you again grasp the false choice presented by the serpent, expecting a different result? Besides a sure sign of insanity, this behavior always leads to the same end of eternal separation of oneself from God and His image.

Motive and Attitude

What drives us? A person strives for worth, assurance, and purpose. These yearnings aren't evil. We have received them in His image. The faulty thinking occurs when we follow the suggestion of the serpent to seek answers in and of ourselves. God has bestowed incredible value on us as well as His assurance and calling. How can there be any more worth than to be the child of the King, and not just any king, but the only King? The promise is built-in. A child is an heir and an heir receives the kingdom from the King. Why do we fight this to seek our own kingdom? We don't have to make ourselves important. We can't. Besides, God took care of that by creating us in His image and then by bringing us back via the life and death of the last Adam. Instead, our purpose is to serve. Our attention is to be 180° from ourselves, on God and our fellowman.

A person must have dignity. It is more than food, clothing, and other possessions. It is how a person is remembered after death. The question is not how I might be remembered after leaving earth. Rather, what will happen to me at the point of life-to-death transition? One doesn't have to die to understand death. We know a little from our own and others' experiences. Some claim to have been to "the other side" briefly, but it cannot be substantiated. The way of the serpent insists we cannot trust God's witness without verification. That kind of thinking appeals to the human ego, but it is an inverted perspective.

Faith is its own proof. The servants with five and two talents understood this. They seized the opportunity to use the knowledge, understanding, and wisdom given them by the Master and by it to increase the Master's resources. They did not make the mistake of the rich fool to think their success was of their own doing or that the returns were for their pleasure alone. God's Word clearly instructs us to be engaged like the first two servants, doing the Master's bidding. If we abdicate entrepreneurial behavior, either because we are too lazy or afraid we can't compete with such as Thomas Edison or Steven Jobs, then we are abandoning the world, like the third servant. That goes against God's intention and directive. We know the outcomes of an economy guided by the way of the serpent: greed, fraud, graft, theft, pyramid schemes, and crony capitalism. We ought no more to abdicate our world to the way of the serpent than the Creator Himself did. His behavior, modeled by the servants with five and two talents, can influence the system to work the way it is intended. It touches our lives in a deeper way than just a job or career. God's directive and the model He provides in His own behavior compel us to be about His business.

More than half of Jesus' parables deal, in one way or another, with His return and our state of preparedness for that fateful day. The same three personalities emerge. The first is a self-assured and arrogant persona that is convinced he or she has everything, including God, all figured out. They convince themselves they are no one's fool. In the parable, however, "fool" is the specific characterization Jesus uses. Such individuals relegate themselves to the position of the greatest fools. Next is the listless and apathetic temperament that Jesus describes as "evil and lazy" in another parable. This one cares for nothing but the handout that will sustain him or her until the next. How they manage to avoid seeing that they are nothing more than panhandlers requires the greatest of self-deceit. Work is for the "poor slob" who can't figure out how to avoid it. They are firmly convinced that everything should be free: free housing, free food, free healthcare, free drugs, then free treatment for substance abuse, and a monthly welfare check that gives them a "fair" income. They are certain they deserve all this and more. They are incapable of thinking of anyone or anything beyond their personal comfort and well-being.

It may seem that the serpent covers both ends of the spectrum and everything between. Yet, there is a third persona that operates on a different plane. This individual is unique, brought back from the way of the serpent to the original relationship with the Creator God. The first Adam didn't resist the serpent and shattered the bonds with the Maker. The broken relationship, however, was restored once and for all by Christ, the last Adam. It is a homecoming to the image of God and it restores our freedom by grace, that we may once again follow the dictates of God's wisdom. In this relationship, a person resists the serpent's temptation and responds with an answer that ignores all apparent evidence to the contrary. This is accomplished by faith. Faith is God's gift, conveyed to each of us because of Jesus' life, death, and resurrection. It is expressed by action, also God's gift, articulated in His charge to subdue and exercise dominion over His creation. That directive is clarified in the Two Tables of the Law, love toward God and our fellowman. Faith and action are attitudinal, empowered by the strength of the Creator Himself and reflective of His image and glory.

There is no tenet to love self. That precept is found in the wisdom of the serpent. It is, in fact, the solitary mandate of the serpent's way. It is the core meaning of "ye shall be as gods." The reason it is so difficult to emulate the third personality type is that humanity remains trapped, though the return to the garden has been accomplished. It is a Jekyll & Hyde existence. A person is forgiven, but sins constantly and receives forgiveness again; he or she sins again and receives forgiveness, and on and on. St. Paul described this constant struggle:

"For what I do is not the good I want to do; no, the evil I do not want to do – this I keep on doing." (Romans 7:19 NIV)

Yet, God has the last word. Luther's advice was to daily "drown" Satan, repeating the answer of faith to all his empty ploys, "You cannot touch me; I am baptized."

Are you ready? The rich fool wasn't. Why not? The warning is simple and straightforward as it always has been. The day of the Lord will come like a thief in the night. Its companion

149

message is short and equally stark: WATCH, and be prepared! Which part of "ready" are we too dense to understand? Many think they have time and perhaps they will. Others try to convince themselves there is no afterlife and eternity. They wonder if this thing about heaven and hell isn't actually an invention to keep mankind in line. They want proof.

A recent article by a physician told of his extended coma during which time he made a visit to heaven that included conversations with God. He was a strong advocate of the scientific method and a skeptic about the existence of a "real" heaven. This experience traumatically shook him and he has reversed his former opinion. Reports of similar incidents are not uncommon. Such first-hand experiences are considered by many as proof of heaven and afterlife. Yet, there is a dichotomy. If "faith is the substance of things hoped for and the evidence of things not seen," as Hebrews 11:1 tells us, then we should require nothing more. Does human reason and personal experience replace what God has revealed in His Word, since the beginning? The encounter of the doctor reminds me of Jesus' parable about the rich man and Lazarus. The rich man, who is in hell, implores God to send Lazarus who is in heaven, to his brothers who are on earth, in order to warn them of the judgment that awaits anyone who lives as their own god. Why aren't the gifts of His Word and faith sufficient? It's as if we need a "sneak peak" to "really believe" what we should already know. Is it so easy for the serpent to slither his way into our lives? We know the way of the serpent and we know the way of the Lord. Which will it be? Most of us don't put ourselves in the place of the rich man. It is not a comfortable feeling. Perhaps we should from time to time so that we are sure to hear the warning. In John 20:29 we read that shortly after the resurrection, Thomas was not convinced until he saw Christ and His scars with his own eyes. Jesus accepts his confession and ours, but admonishes us by pronouncing special blessings on those who believe without seeing. Faith has more weight than evidence (Proof of Heaven by Eben Alexander, M.D. To be published by Simon & Schuster, Inc., 2012 by Eben Alexander III, M.D.)

To be ready for judgment is the state in which God wants us. That final event occurs in one of two ways. The first is Jesus' return to earth on Judgment Day. It marks the end of "the age." The second and most likely way we will experience it is by dying, though we will also be present at the former. At death, God immediately pronounces His verdict and our eternal fate. *"And as it is appointed for men once to die, but after this the judgment." (Hebrews 9:27)* It is the central lesson of the parable about the rich fool. It is one of the reasons for its prominence in this book. At the end of the parable God informs the rich fool, ready or not, that he has no time left. He wasn't ready. Are you?

If this is our goal, then how do we get there? St. Paul sharply rebuked a group of people because they were sitting on a mountaintop awaiting the Lord's return. If that is our "ready" then we're not. Neither are we at liberty to take our own life to hasten the judgment. There are countless ways NOT to be ready. Follow the way of the serpent and we are guaranteed to NOT be ready. There is only one way to be ready and that is the way of the Lord. Look again to the beginning. After creating Adam and Eve, God placed them into the garden and charged them to "have dominion" over creation. His intent and will for them – and for us – is to work. God illustrates His attitude toward work by His own engagement in creation. Genesis 2:3 tells us that God rested from His work of creation on the seventh day. Paul admonishes us in 2 Thessalonians 3:10 that if a person is not ready to work, then he should not expect to be fed as a result of someone else's work. God invented work and sanctified it, so we know it is a good thing.

God's intent and will is for us to work in His garden and make no mistake about it, it is still His garden, no matter the lies of Satan or the world around us. We are to embrace it with the same creativity and energy that we witness in His own work of creation. His free resources of knowledge, understanding, and wisdom are accessible to everyone, but those who choose the way of the Lord have an insurmountable advantage. While those who follow the way of the serpent can sometimes be intimidating, their horizons are bound to earth. Their ill-fated delusion about being their own god distorts their spiritual "GPS" readings. In perpetual confusion, they confuse the means and the end. Echoing Einstein's definition of insanity, they repeat the serpent-inspired self-serving behavior, expecting to somehow achieve inner satisfaction. It won't happen! Those returned to the way of the Lord recognize God's resources. We know the limitless reservoir from which they flow, and understand the means has an end to be fulfilled. Our relationship with God is "the substance of things hoped for." We don't work for that end. It has already been given to us. We work because of it. Like the servants who received five and two talents, we don't have to stress out over, or even consider, failure.

Some complain that America's leadership is placing not only free enterprise, but freedom itself in jeopardy. We see evidence that in order to succeed, one must curry favor with those in power and get ahead by practicing "crony capitalism". At times, we are sorely tempted to throw up our hands, because all is lost, but we can't allow the serpent, who toils diligently, to delude us with his alternate reality. At one end we see those who seem to have figured out entrepreneurial behavior. Their business success seems explosive and unstoppable. Their personal wealth just keeps growing. Or, a gifted athlete determines his prowess is sourced in himself alone. As he prances in the end zone, or whatever venue, he seems unbeatable: "I'm #1." The emotions reflected by these individuals are appealing. They make people appear invincible, especially to themselves. Yet, they only cause overconfidence and augment arrogance. Without realizing it, more likely not caring, they become clones of the rich fool. At the other end we find the "evil and lazy" ones, who have no integrity, respect, or regard for their own talents or those of anyone else. They seek redistribution of wealth others have created, because "it seems only fair" to them and to the politicians who covet their votes. They feel some sort of "righteous anger" when they are regaled with claims that if the rich take too much of the economic "pizza pie" the rest will have only an empty pizza box on which to chew. What a pathetic equivocation. It's easy to recognize the third servant from the parable of the talents. We may feel, at times, like "chucking" this messy world. After all, we tell ourselves, God must be ready to rid Himself of all the bad "stuff" and all the bad people. That is not how God operates and we know it. He didn't rid Himself of the "mess" in the beginning and He doesn't do it now. His intent and will is steady. He is the same yesterday, today, and forever. Follow Him, not your own self-god. "Have dominion" in His garden.

That was the reality in the beginning and it is the reality today. We are not at liberty to desert the world and attendant evils any more than the servant with one talent. God did not desert the world when humans rejected Him to follow the way of the serpent. Neither does God intend for us to desert the world: not to live as Adam and Eve after the fall, but as the "last" Adam, in faith and action. God has given us free access to His resources of knowledge, understanding, and wisdom. Many who continue to

153

follow the way of the serpent happily use this vestige of God's image, even though they are unable to recognize the presence and gift of God's resources. They lie to themselves that rational thought is something that materializes from air. That, however, is not the point. Rather, how dare we NOT use them to the greatest extent of the talents God has given to each of us? If we follow the way of the Lord, we know the outcome of heeding His call. It does not matter whether we possess one, two, or five talents. We have received His gifts for this purpose. God Himself will take care of the results of our work. He is, and the serpent is not, the judge of us, our work, and those around us.

Opportunity

Opportunities abound. They are summarized for our enlightenment in the two tables of the Law: love God and love your fellowman. *"...there is no commandment greater than these." (Mark 12:31NIV).* The parable of the Good Samaritan is about opportunity. The priest, the Levite, and the Samaritan had the same opportunity. Since Jesus begins by saying, "a man was going down from Jerusalem," it is logical to assume the victim was of pure Jewish lineage. The first traveler was frightened and the second didn't want to waste his time. The third, a member of the impure and despised Samaritan clan understood God's definition (first entrepreneurial trait) of neighbor. Thoughts of danger and inconvenience were dismissed to do (second trait) the right thing. He tended to the man's physical and psychological needs as he might hope to be treated were their places exchanged. The needs of our neighbor don't occur according to a schedule, certainly not our schedule. Yet, they are part of our pilgrim journey and if we don't recognize them as such, perhaps we need glasses to re-invert our vision to God's right side up posture.

Relationships

In creation, the Creator modeled the entrepreneurial behavior humans are to emulate. God laid out the purpose and plan He wants mankind to follow. The entrepreneurial behavior modeled by God is superior to any innate ability to succeed in business. His greater gift is a spiritual lesson, an understanding that all aspects of our daily lives, not just our work and careers, are to be filled to the full and guided to eternal success by the Spirit of this Divine Model. *"...I have come that they may have life, and have it to the full." (John 10:10 NIV)*

The entirety of God's dealings with and blessings to us are one after another, instance after instance of entrepreneurial behavior. St. Paul reminds us that *"...God is at work in you to will and to act according to His good purpose."(Philippians 2:13 NIV)* You just may have noticed that *"to will"* is the first entrepreneurial trait and *"to act"* is the second. The will is faith to act. Paul reminds us that salvation is more than a gift to be received and then, as it were, left on the shelf. That was the failure of the servant with one talent. Faith and salvation are expressed in a process that includes active participation. Faith and action cannot be separated.

God's expectation is for us to create and work on and through interpersonal relationships. The First Table of the Law tells us about the relationship God seeks with us. The Second tells us about the relationships God wants us to have with our fellow-humans. It is no big surprise that interpersonal relationships operate through the same character traits found in all entrepreneurial behavior. Faith and trust (risk-taking) are the cornerstones of relationships. Second, interpersonal relationships function by virtue of actions (initiative) toward and on behalf of the two parties involved. The original spousal relationship was ordained by the

Creator before the temptation of the serpent. It is the only post-creation (but, pre-sin) ordination of God not enacted as an antidote. This makes marriage a special relationship as it reflects the behavior ordained in a perfect garden.

Because of God's entrepreneurial action after humans fell to the lure of the serpent, His Son became a human and lived the life intended of the first Adam. God realizes the relationship He desires in the "second Adam." This "last Adam" won our salvation, once and for all, and God, once again, has the relationship He sought (we didn't seek it) with man, from the beginning. Jesus' life on earth demonstrates how we are to fulfill the human side of the relationship. It is only as God's redeemed children that we are able to reciprocate. This occurs when we "put on Christ" and are back to our original condition. "Putting on Christ" happens in baptism and it is this state that we strive for every day as we drown Satan with the remembrance of our baptism. The relationship between the Creator and each of us plays out in a partnership to subdue and have dominion over the earth. This does not mean a relationship of dominance, but of service.

The manner in which God enables us to realize a relationship with Him is the same way we are to build relationships with our fellow-humans. "Love your neighbor as yourself." Relationships are not like bank accounts as many treat them: you know, a deposit when you do someone a favor and a withdrawal when someone does a favor for you. Some cultures practice this to the point that a relationship "account balance" can actually require someone's life. Any time you want to see the correct way to react to a particular situation in a relationship, simply imagine that God is the other party in question. In a relationship, we do not count the cost. We simply act in love and respect toward each other the way

God acts toward us. As with all aspects of God's image, we are to serve the Master and our fellowman.

Relationships are entrepreneurial, consisting entirely of trust and action. Communication is the vehicle by which relationships are facilitated. Interpersonal communication is the "sine qua non" of relationships. There are many unanswered questions. How did God communicate with man and woman in the garden? Were methods of communication oral or nonverbal? Perhaps it was telepathic. What does it mean when the Gospel-writer John and others refer to Jesus as the "Word"? Why did God endow us with the ability to communicate? What about our use of communication for the wrong purposes, like when we curse? Are we abominating Christ, who is the Word, when we do that? Will communication ability be taken from those eternally separated from God? The absence of answers requires entrepreneurial faith.

Giving and Receiving

The way of the serpent doesn't acknowledge forgiveness, except perhaps in the strictest sense of exchange. Giving and receiving are found nowhere in its lexicon. The way of the serpent seeks only to stockpile what is already possessed and to appropriate whatever else is coveted. It is only when confiscation doesn't work that negotiation and bargaining are employed.

The lifeblood of relationships is embodied in giving and receiving, mutual and constant actions in which the two parties engage. Paul G. Bretscher, yet again, provides this insight in numerous writings. Giving, the first component, is the action by which a person transfers something in his or her possession to the other party. At times the gift is tangible, like money or other physical goods. More often, however, it is intangible, like kindness,

157

sympathy, assistance, care, praise, and encouragement. The Samaritan made use of physical gifts like bandages and ointments to help the robbery victim. He probably used water to wash the wounds and to give the victim a drink. Then he placed the injured person on his own beast of burden to transport him safely to the inn, where he also used his own money to pay the innkeeper. He also gave a number of intangible things to the victim like comfort, encouragement, and assurance that he need not worry about his immediate safety and later his healing. It is likely the victim and the Samaritan established a lasting interpersonal relationship. The Samaritan's actions are the embodiment of giving. God's gift of His image and then His own Son are incomparable examples of giving. (Bretscher, Paul G. <u>The Mystery of Oneness</u>. Copyright Parish Leadership Seminars, Inc., 1980. pp. 36-37).

The second action in relationships is receiving. Everyone knows and understands the phrase, "Give and Take." It is usually associated with how we get through various situations in life. The action of "taking", however, is not the counterpart to "giving." Contrary to thinking that reflects the way of the serpent, "taking" is not the reciprocal of "giving" in an interpersonal relationship. Whether you think about the gifts of mind, talents, and abilities received from God, or the gifts received in a human relationship, the complementary action to giving is receiving, not taking. A relationship is not, as typified by one popular self-help "guru," comparable to a bank account in which a deposit is made when you do a favor for someone and a withdrawal is taken when someone does a favor for you.

It is not difficult to understand the concept of receiving, so long as the gift we receive is of an enjoyable and positive nature. But what about something that is unwanted and negative, like a physical slap, an unwanted argument with a spouse, a confrontation with a child, a dispute with a coworker, or a negative evaluation from a supervisor? How should we receive these? Concerning unwanted gifts, remember that Job observed, *"Shall we accept good from God and not trouble?" (Job 2:10 NIV)* Learn from Christ: when He received criticism and other "evil" from those who opposed Him and sought His death, He did not retaliate. Instead, He "received" (or accepted) all disapproval and reproach as well as death from his tormenters.

Try this experiment: for an hour, just sixty minutes, "receive" all the criticism, comments, and other subjective evaluations from your spouse or a close friend without responding in any way, other than to "receive" them. It is remarkably difficult. Life is not about "give and take." It is about giving and receiving.

The manner by which God enables us to realize a relationship with Him is the same way that we are to build relationships with our fellowman. "Love your neighbor as yourself." The very same entrepreneurial and generous fashion God employs to build relationships with us, through faith and action, is the same method we are to use to establish and build relationships with each other. When you want to see the correct way to react to a particular situation in a relationship, simply imagine that Jesus is the other party in question ("you did it unto me"). In a relationship, we do not count the cost, but simply act in love toward one another the way God acts toward us.

Forgiveness

The greatest act of giving and receiving is forgiveness, a truly unique part of God's image. It remained hidden until sin brought it to light. It surprised the serpent, who thought God's warning of the death sentence for sinning was the final answer. It also surprised the humans, who have been poor recipients and practitioners ever since. What might have happened, had Adam and Eve fallen on their faces to seek forgiveness after falling to the lure of the serpent? Unfortunately, we will never know, but it is interesting to think about. Human reasoning is still contaminated by the tree of the knowledge of good and evil.

The fact of God's forgiveness does not depend on our acceptance. Our sins, as well as all sins of all people of all time, were paid for when Jesus died the awful death on the cross.

"And He died for all, that those who live should no longer live for themselves but for Him who died for them and was raised again." *(2 Corinthians 5:15 NIV)*

He gives us the power to claim forgiveness. It is the only way it can be received. What a waste people make of it when they choose to refuse it and remain in the way of the serpent. It is, yet again, the servant with one talent refusing to be engaged in the Way of the Lord, who tells us at once the "what for" of forgiveness. What does it mean to be forgiven? What actions does it evoke? Forgiveness is certainly the most significant gift we receive in our relationship with the Creator. By His grace we now know to fall on our faces before the Creator every time we allow the serpent to reinvert us in his way.

Besides serving God, we are to serve our fellowman. The greatest act we perform in carrying out the Second Table of God's Law is the gift of forgiveness. It mirrors God's forgiveness. Giving it to others is God-like. Yet, there is another aspect of forgiveness that might slip past us. It has to do with what happens in us when we engage in the act of forgiveness. When we engage in an act of forgiveness, it removes our own burden. An acquaintance related the following incident. He was involved in his neighborhood association and became embroiled in a dispute with another association member. His fellow-member had said something to which my friend took umbrage. The final comment about this flare-up was, "I'll show him. I won't forgive him!" I asked whether the other person was aware of the latest episode in their battle, to which my friend said, "No. Why do you ask?" Who is affected by the refusal to forgive? The obvious burden was on my friend and the refusal to forgive increased the load.

When we forgive, we need to make sure to also accept God's forgiveness to ourselves.

There is also a positive side to forgiveness. Consider all we receive from the Creator. Besides our being and all we receive from the gift of God's image, we have also received His entire creation. He doesn't require us to pay back the cost of anything. To receive a glimpse of God's positive action toward us in this regard, think about your children. How much have you given them? How much are you prepared to continue giving them? Would you want or expect a child to pay you back? Neither does God. There is a petition in the Lord's Prayer: "forgive us our trespasses as we forgive those who trespass against us." Trespasses are generally thought of from their negative standpoint. One meaning of a trespass, beyond sin, is "debt." The debt our children owe for all they receive from us is "good" debt. It is the same as we owe God for all we receive in His image.

What will you do with God's gift of forgiveness?

Relationships give purpose to entrepreneurial behavior. The object of that purpose can be found in the two Tables of the Law: God and neighbor. That's it, that's all: nothing about self. First, the relationship with God: His desire for this relationship was so great that He altered His creation mode to make humans the "crown" of His creation. This relationship was so dear that He amended His process of justice and judgment when humans chose the alternate wisdom of the serpent. He sent His son to substitute Himself and suffer the consequences of our sin. That is the ultimate exchange in any relationship. Jesus said that there is no greater "love" than one person giving up life for the sake of another person. This is not merely a cliché, but the source of all our actions, directed toward God and our fellowman.

The Good Samaritan gives flesh and blood to God's directive. Looking at this parable, attention is usually focused on the attitudes and actions of, first, the Levite, next the priest, and finally the Samaritan. The Levite and the priest are like the third servant in the parable of the talents. They are evil (self-centered) and lazy. The Samaritan uses his rational capacity to tend the wounds of the victim and takes action to assist in his healing and the prevention of additional attacks. He is the personification of the two faithful servants in the parable of the talents. But, just who is the victim? For sure, he is the one God calls our "neighbor." There is more. Jesus gives us a list of commendable acts of those He declares blessed and inheritors of His Father's kingdom and then concludes: *"...whatever you did for one of the least of these brothers and sisters of mine, you did it for me." (Matthew 25:40 NIV)* It is as if Jesus, Himself, is the victim to whom the Samaritan exhibits faith and action. The deeds by which we express faith and action to our fellowman are demonstrations of our faith and action toward God.

At a day-to-day level, this principle gives practical meaning to God's directive to have dominion over His creation. The essence of this task is expressed every time we use our rational capacity to uncover new things or to create new products and processes from materials God has placed in the universe at our disposal. It includes events like the control of fire for useful purposes, discovery of the new world, or the first time a child whistles. It also includes the development of crude oil into fuel, the invention of the light bulb, or a child's first finger painting. An important part of mankind's dominion over creation of new products like gasoline or nuclear power, is the parallel development of new processes to protect the environment. The toughest element in this lesson, however, is not what we do and are capable of doing, but to understand why and toward whom our actions are to be directed. Creation of the silicon chip was a momentous event. The God-created substance of sand was combined with human rational capacity to create a product that is fueling America's technology age. It is also creating untold wealth. This doesn't happen because of government, the labor class, or society. It happens because of individuals who use God's visible resources of physical matter along with God's invisible resources of knowledge, understanding, and wisdom. The parable of the rich fool tells the same story, but with a really unhappy ending. The moral: *"This is how it will be with anyone who stores up things for himself but is not rich toward God" (Luke 12:21 NIV)*. It is the way of the serpent. Yet, it doesn't have to be that way. Because of the "last" Adam our experience can have the alternate ending of the way of the Lord.

After telling the parable of the wealthy landowner, Jesus applies it to His listeners.

In His Image

"Have you never read in the Scriptures? The stone the builders rejected has become the capstone; the Lord has done this, and it is marvelous in our eyes. Therefore I tell you that the kingdom of God will be taken away from you and given to a people who will produce its fruit. He who falls on this stone will be broken to pieces, but he on whom it falls will be crushed" (Matthew 22:42-44 NIV).

The religious leaders thought, by virtue of their genealogy and status as religious leaders, that the kingdom of God was theirs. We must be careful not to fall into the same trap. We think we have a right to God's blessing because we live in a Christian land, or we live among Christians, or we go to church, or our parents are Christians. We feel we have appropriated the blessings of God by our own virtue. Although we worship as a family or a congregation, God looks into the heart of each person. In turn, each must individually heed God's Word, call on the name of the Lord, and accept Him, through God's gift of grace, as his or her personal Lord.

Imagine millions of people exercising God's directive to have dominion over His creation by combining physical matter in His creation with the invisible resources of knowledge, understanding, and wisdom. The potential for countless and continuing creations is not only possible, it is inevitable. God has invited us to undertake this calling and gives us the resources and tools to accomplish it. We think small because we are finite. God is infinite. What are we waiting for?

Our response depends on our interpersonal relationship with God and with each other. It is about faith and action. And, like our relationship with God and with each other, it occurs one person at a time.

Chapter 9

Discussion Questions

1. Discuss what you think about the statement: "The restoration of the relationship with the Creator restores entrepreneurial freedom and free will."

2. The author said, "Like Abraham, we are led by an entrepreneurial God who empowers us to trust and obey, as well as emulate His own behavior." What might this look like in your life now and into the future?

3. "As Christians, our motivation and attitude is not so much about free will, but a redeemed and restored will." Contrast how these different vantage points can be seen in the world and in the church.

4. What fears might disrupt entrepreneurial behavior in your life?

5. Jesus' return is an emphasis of the Biblical parables. For what areas of your life does the return of Jesus bring a sense of urgency?

Chapter Ten

Entrepreneurial Creative Power

It has been the endeavor of the writer to provide, in a Christian context, a resource for readers that fosters and supports creativity and action. It is not the intent nor is it possible to dictate what specific moves might be undertaken. Neither is it the intent to instigate a popular or political movement or statement.

This is, however, an exhortation and an opportunity to reflect on the blessings Americans have received from the Creator. The faith of our immigrant ancestors, in God and themselves, meshed ideally with the cultural and political structures created by our founders in the Declaration of Independence, the Constitution, and the Bill of Rights. Their vision and aspirations continue to give hope and substance to those from around the world who seek freedom and happiness. Desire for freedom is a timeless value. It is never outdated or antiquated. This entrepreneurial spirit and determination is as strong today as when the first American colonies were founded. It is the root and core of the phenomenon known as the great American Experiment. Its prodigy is American Exceptionalism.

Now it's our turn.

Entrepreneurial Behavior

Noted earlier, the character traits of Christian faith are inescapably entrepreneurial. It is the behavior demonstrated by God from the beginning and into our own time.

1.   Faith (risk-taking): faith is the ultimate risk. *"Now faith is being sure of what we hope for and certain of what we do not see." (Hebrews 11:1 NIV)*

2.   Independent initiative: faith motivates actions that reflect one's relationship with God. These are an individual matter between God and you, without reliance on any human person (including yourself) or agency. *"...continue to work out your salvation with fear and trembling, for it is God who works in you to will and to act according to His good purpose." (Philippians 2:12-13 NIV)*

The issue is not whether the image of God resides in you. Everyone has it. The only question is centered on motivation and attitude. Are you guided by the way of the Lord or by the way of the serpent? A non-response is an answer, the same as the servant with one talent. The rich fool also misread the gifts he received and assumed success was his own doing. Both personalities spring from the same self-centeredness and pride. Indifference to God's gifts renders both useless: *"...I am about to spit you out of my mouth." (Revelation 3:16 NIV)* Your own response is between you and God. Parents cannot answer, nor spouse, the church, friends, teachers, the government, nor anyone or anything else.

Mankind had everything, freely given by a caring Creator. In a moment of thoughtless desire and pride, humans rejected their Maker. By this action, they relegated mankind to life under the tree of the knowledge of good and evil. This makes survival of the fittest the only rule and norm. As a result, humans are in a prison of their own making, trying to seize whatever is desired (lust) and to reject anything perceived to be undesirable (fear).

So, God did the unthinkable. At least to us mortals it is inconceivable. He sent His Son, referred to as the last Adam, because He sustained the interpersonal relationship with the Creator, an expectation the first Adam did not fulfill. There is no need for another, hence the "last."

There is more to the story, however, than just a perfect life that, of itself, does nothing more than underscore human failure. The serpent was certain of victory. He should have known better, for he was dealing with a force immeasurably superior to his first victim. The last Adam didn't merely live a substitute life, but also took upon Himself our penalty as well. *"The wages of sin is death..."* (Romans 6:23a NIV) God's justice cannot be evaded, not by humans and not by God. It demands a "payday," so to speak. The last Adam consorted with sinners. His actions condemned Him as a sinner. Don't put Jesus on a pedestal that cannot reconcile His death as a sinner. If He is not the sinner, then we are and must face a sentence we cannot survive. *"God made Him who knew no sin to be sin for us,"* (2Corinthians 5:21a NIV). He stepped into the breach between the righteousness of God and the serpent's tyranny. The last Adam then received, on our behalf, the consequences. *"...when you eat of it you will surely die."* (Genesis 2:17 NIV)

This was not (wink-wink, nod-nod) play acting, but actual "in place of" death. *"...the Lord has laid on Him the iniquity of us all."* (Isaiah 53:6b NIV) While the reality was terrifying, perhaps the most chilling aspect was the unknown. Since Jesus was in a human state, He did not know what awaited Him on the other side of the cross. If He did, the crucifixion was a hoax. All He had was God's promise, the Word of His Father, the same word and promise we receive. That was sufficient for Jesus as He remained faithful to the relationship. The substitute died! Imagine that! He

169

died to fulfill God's system of justice. But in His death was hidden the power to defeat the serpent. It restored for all time the trust and interpersonal bond between God and mankind.

God intervened with an action-plan that satisfied His perfect justice and restored the freedom He had bestowed at creation, only to have it squandered. Death is what we have earned. Life is what we receive. *"...the gift of God is eternal life...."* *(Romans 6:23b NIV)* When you once again are in the interpersonal relationship with God (that's what redemption means), you might sometimes feel burdened by sin, to the point you don't feel saved. Do you feel saved? It matters not if you "feel" saved. It matters only what the last Adam did. Remember this when you don't feel saved.

This isn't the only "death to life" story in Scripture. An agricultural metaphor from St. Paul helps us understand. When a seed is planted, it rots and decays. Yet, from the apparent death a new plant grows and produces a multitude of new seeds. Fortunately, one needn't comprehend it to enjoy a dinner roll or Danish pastry. Through the death of a substitute, our new life is created and produces "new seeds." God's intent is for each of us to be returned to an interpersonal bond with Him. We enjoy this relationship so long as we are under His protection and care, in a state of grace. Though we are still sinful, His grace frees us from the consequences. This is faith, the first entrepreneurial principle.

The second entrepreneurial precept is found in His omnipotent action. Just observe what He did in creation. He used His knowledge, understanding, and wisdom to design, organize, and bring about the entire enterprise. The power revealed in creation is truly overwhelming. Have you ever examined the "action" (work) element of creation?

"By the seventh day God had finished the work He had been doing" (Genesis 2:2 NIV).

Does God work? That's what He tells us. Some imagine God saying, or effortlessly thinking, "Let there be" and it was. After working He sanctified His rest on the seventh day. Even today, a day of rest is recognized. More significant, however, is the fact that God worked. Work is not a consequence of the serpent's way, after all. God sanctified the work He did in creation. Contrary to the example of millions, work is a blessing of God's image. St. Paul tells us:

"If a man will not work, he shall not eat." (II Thessalonians 3:10 NIV)

Not only are we to "sanctify the Holy Day", but our work as well. Work is a part of the gift we have received with God's image.

If this is how God revealed Himself in creation, what does it mean in our own lives? For one, it shows us that entrepreneurial behavior wasn't discovered or invented by some clever people to establish an economic system. Free enterprise has facilitated the emergence of entrepreneurial behavior in business. That is great! If you're not already part of a creative work enterprise, don't ignore opportunities. Immeasurably more significant, however, it is the behavior modeled for us by God as the manner in which we are to live and work on a daily basis and in every aspect of our lives. Not only is the behavior of entrepreneurs like Edison and Ford a

171

manifestation of the "image of God" in them, the same entrepreneurial DNA dwells in each of us. This is not wishful thinking, an opinion, or a supposition. God says to have dominion over His creation. Faith and action are the two traits of entrepreneurial behavior and this same motive and attitude are to be the substance and sustenance of our lives, every day. We received a full measure of intelligence from God. It includes, but isn't limited to business and commercial enterprise. Creation of wealth is an appropriate use of God's resources, given to us by use of the knowledge, understanding, and wisdom exercised in our minds. It becomes unholy only when we determine it to be our own doing, motivated by greed and domination of our fellowman.

Humans are still victimized by their decision to follow the way of the serpent, believing they can be their own god. We live one day at a time like recovering alcoholics. It is sin from which we are recovering. In the mode of "recovering sinners" we are gifted God's knowledge, understanding, and wisdom in order to have dominion and recreate God's world continuously in our lives and in the lives of those around us.

Faith and Action

So, let's get at it. As they say, it isn't rocket science. Jesus Himself models the behavior. Martin Luther, in his Maundy Thursday sermon in 1544, noted that although He is the greatest of Lords, Jesus does what slaves and servants do. He washes His disciples' feet. He laid aside His glory (we have that same "glory" in our redeemed state) and ignored it. He never abused it for His own pride, power, or advantage, but used it for the good of His servants. We are to do the same. We should never exalt ourselves because of our gifts, never abuse them as an occasion for pride, but serve our neighbor with them to the limit of the power bestowed on us by God.

Every human is different from every other human, not just by gender, ethnicity, and fingerprints, but in every way one may or may not imagine. Do you think the parable of the talents is trying to tell us that some people are better than others? Certainly not! It means your make-up is different from every other person who has ever lived. Kenyans win more marathons than runners from other countries. The best camera lenses are made by Japanese and Germans. Children of Indian descent win a disproportionate number of spelling bees. Women are different from men in significant ways. Look around you. Even by casual comparison it is easy to see how different everyone is. If you are a parent of more than one, you will quickly acknowledge this even if you have identical twins. Faith is part of the image of God. It is the DNA that makes the relationship between God and a person unique from all others, of all time. One size does not fit all. God deals with each person individually. How's that for value?

There are, however, some ways in which we are alike. We're all sinners. Jesus died for us all. How did we come to be the person we are with the talents we have? None of us did a thing to earn or deserve the talents we boast, whether five, two, one, or however many. Perhaps among the most deluded are those with great talent, who think and act as though they are the source of their own gifts. The source is no mystery if we understand the parable of talents.

So, what are we to do with our talents? How are we to deal with the gifts we receive from God? What is NOT to be done is answered unambiguously and bluntly. The rich fool arrogantly tried to stockpile his blessings. The inconvenient truth for him was to be called to judgment that very night. The servant with one talent did nothing, not even engage minimally in the society to which he belonged. He then compounded his error by complaining that the master was unfair to expect anything from him. The master called him "wicked and lazy" and cast him into darkness where expectations are limited to "weeping and gnashing of teeth."

Don't the punishments in both parables seem a bit harsh? Is God really so demanding? The quick answer is YES! Virtually all Scriptural references to haughtiness and slothfulness are met with condemnation. Just what do these behaviors deserve, if not God's contempt? What does a sinner deserve? Are some sins more damning than others? Certainly, some misdeeds cause more earthly harm than others, but there is no distinction in God's declaration, "the wages of sin is death." Sin is sin. There is no such state as "slightly damned" or "somewhat saved."

Since we're on the subject, have you ever thought about the reality of hell, separation from God? It seems possible that those in hell do not enjoy even the vestiges of God's image. It removes a number of God's gifts we enjoy on earth: joy, peace, goodness, generosity, patience, faithfulness, and contentment, to name a few. How about the gift of communication? Is it absent in hell? It is impossible to contemplate the eternal vexation and anger of being unable to communicate. But, perhaps the greatest and most infuriating reality and recrimination of hell is that salvation is free. The lament that redemption is "not fair" is correct. We can only receive it as pure gift.

Another lesson regarding the misuse of talents comes from the parable of the rich fool. He was not faulted because he used

God's talents, but because he took God's gifts for granted with no thought of their source or their proper use. Interestingly, this parable does not attribute to the rich man any of the actions that resulted in the "bumper" or "windfall" crop, not even ownership of the land. Jesus tells His listeners and us, *"The ground of a certain rich man yielded an abundant harvest."* Rich means, I believe, an abundance of talents, which gives broader application to the story. Jesus' choice of the word "ground" may be intended to help us understand everything is God's doing: owning the land (talent), strategizing a plan (talent), implementing the plan (talent), reaping benefits (talent), even growing (talent) and harvesting (talent). This puts the athlete's boast, "I'm the greatest" in the right perspective. The final condemnation is especially pointed:

"This is how it will be with anyone who stores up things for himself, but is not rich toward God." (Luke 12:21 NIV)

The reason God gives us (they're His, not ours) talents and gifts is for them to be used for God and for our fellowman, not for ourselves. So, how should we understand an entrepreneur who creates a super-successful business and becomes rich beyond measure? There is nothing wrong with the creation of wealth. What is wrong, however, is to amass earthly treasure and then repeat the sin of the rich fool.

Two self-centered individuals, the rich fool and the servant with one talent. Both were arrogant. One attempted to dominate his fellowman with fame and fortune. The other manipulated those around him into serving him. Neither had time for or gave the slightest thought to God or to his fellowman. It is the way of the serpent. Two different outcomes, but the eternal consequences are the same. They confused the end and the means. The end, as in "light at the end of the tunnel," is eternity. It is an interpersonal bond and partnership with the Creator that never ends. The means, as in "God's resources," is closely associated with motive and attitude, which constrain us to use the entrepreneurial gifts (talents) we have received for the sole purpose of serving God and our fellowman. The rich fool and the servant with one talent both had the capacity to understand the difference. Yet, in the self-centered way of the serpent, both misconstrued the means for the end. In their minds, the means was the end.

The servants with five and two talents made entrepreneurial use of their gifts according to the Master's training and expectation. Both were commended and invited to share in the Master's happiness. The meaning is quite transparent. First, we are to be "about our Father's business" and second, we should not confuse the end and the means. The end is eternity with the Master. The means is the use of God's talents (entrepreneurial gifts) that we have received for service to God and our fellowman.

The servants with five and two talents responded entrepreneurially to their opportunities. It was in the power of the third servant to choose the same. He didn't. Leading with the first character trait of entrepreneurs, the servants with five and two talents exercised their faith and trusted their instincts and other invisible resources that their master had provided: knowledge, understanding, and wisdom. They didn't wait for the Master to return and approve their plans and strategies. Without delay, they applied an entrepreneur's second character trait by acting on the plans they had devised. Both were commended and invited to share the Master's happiness. It is significant that the there is no mention of fear about failure. An important aspect of entrepreneurial behavior is that once an action plan is devised and implemented it is a waste of time and energy to worry about decisions that have been made. A prudent manager monitors and makes adjustments as appropriate, but the Master has trained his servants to look at all pertinent information, make what appears to be the best decision, and then trust their instincts.

Entrepreneurial behavior is no more and no less than our possession of God's capacity to be creative and to take action to subdue and have dominion over creation. That's it: the directive to "have dominion" consists of faith and action. God has given us free access to His resources of knowledge, understanding, and wisdom. Faith, the first of the two entrepreneurial elements, is our rational capacity to engage in abstract thought to be creative and devise plans. People like Thomas Edison and Steven Jobs did and still do this, as well as the gardener caring for my lawn or a child taking a parent's hand to cross a busy street. Action, the second element, is individual initiative that enables us to accomplish the objectives of creative thought, the first element.

Getting Faith Right: Follow the Model

When mankind rebelled and chose the way of the serpent, God did not destroy him or turn His back on creation. Instead, He sought to restore the relationship. How else can His recovery plan be explained? His will is for us to mirror the faith (trust) and action (initiative) He models. He is the authentic model. We are returned to this relationship, one-to-one. The idea proposed by the serpent that we can be our own gods is self-centered and self-destructive. Our attempts to use the serpent's bogus model are tragicomic failures even before we act on them.

Jesus is candid about expectations: *"Be perfect, therefore, as your heavenly Father is perfect" (Matthew 5:48 NIV).* He also tells any who would be His disciple that *"...he must deny himself and take up his cross daily and follow me. (Luke 9:23 NIV)* These things are not said in jest or hypothetically. He says what He means. The self-centered way of the serpent is to be aborted. How utterly impossible! Isn't God unreasonable to make such a demand? After all, we're only human. We may be correct, but the real problem is flawed reasoning. If anyone knows we're defective, it is God. We are not perfect at any level and our attempts at such are contemptible. The attempt to define their own perfection and create their own world is where the trouble began in the first place. The only thing accomplished was death, physical and eternal.

The issue goes deeper. When Adam and Eve attempted to create their own reality, they acted alone and separate from each other. If truth is light and sin is darkness, then sin can only be committed in "blackness." It prohibits cooperative action. The fact that both humans participated only meant that two people acted separately and alone. When free will chose to disobey, it was a one-person decision. It always is. Yet, humans were not created to function alone. Integral to the reality of God is His intent to have an interpersonal bond with each person. Creation of a mate was an extension of that link. To be in a relationship with God reflects His own preference. God is not alone, but composed of Father, Son, and Spirit – yet One God. Contemplating the creation of the first human, He uses the plural pronoun: *"Let **us** make man in **our** image" (Genesis 1:26 NIV)*. This is vital to the divine model. We have received His attributes so we can be connected to Him. From there, this capacity extends to our mate, then to others, and finally to all creation.

God's seemingly unreasonable expectation and demand for perfection takes place in the context of this interpersonal bond.

Humans have been endowed with the means, motive, and opportunity to carry it out. God demonstrates His own faith and action in creation and within that revelation is the power for humans to also carry it out. Earlier we noted God's faith, though it may better be understood as confidence. He has faith in Himself and His creative competence and capacity to get things done. Look at the world and universe in which you exist, conceived by the mind of God and created by His power. God also has faith in us. If it is not so, why did He create us in His image? Humans are created to be and remain in relationship with God, who seeks this vital link with each of us. He trusts mankind, the crown of creation and made in His image, to be an equal partner in a deep bond of divine friendship, creativity, and energy.

Getting Freedom Right: Recovering American Exceptionalism

At first blush, the freedom we seek in our daily lives as Americans appears unconnected to the freedom enjoyed by those returned to the interpersonal bond with their Creator. For those who are trapped in the way of the serpent, such thought is nonsense. Yet, if liberty is granted us by divine provenance, the two share a significant link. We simply cannot have it both ways. Once we comprehend the exceptionalism we have received as children and heirs of the Creator, our objective of re-energizing America takes on a different perspective. America's founders were men of faith, driven by a vision of liberty and equal treatment under the law. They believed that freedom is not grounded in human capability. It cannot be conferred by one person on another. It presupposes divine provenance. John Adams cautioned: "Our Constitution was made only for moral and upright people of faith. It is wholly inadequate for the government of any other." Absent its divine author, freedom loses its authenticity.

In His Image

Freedom is not a collection of idealistic truisms that operate like a romantic tale of courage and chivalry. George Washington, Thomas Jefferson, Benjamin Franklin, and Patrick Henry stepped deliberately into the chasm between tyranny and freedom. "Give me liberty or give me death" was no idle boast by Patrick Henry. American patriots knew if they lost the war, King George III would hang the leaders and oppress them all. Yet, they also knew they were spot-on in their belief about the centrality of liberty and freedom to mankind's highest ideal and achievement.

Besides its high cost, freedom demands diligence and hard work. The founders were resolute and insistent about the way American democracy should function. Freedom and democracy as well as its progeny, free enterprise, weren't created and don't sustain themselves with the snap of a finger. They require vision, persistence, and diligence. Some think America is on the cusp of a post-democracy and post-free enterprise era. Those who favor such a transformation constantly chip away at the edges to undermine and discredit the principles and values that have shaped its success and prosperity. One of their primary arguments is that America's founding ideals and documents are obsolete and in need of modernization and revision.

Freedom is never passé or obsolete and those who believe in "Life, Liberty, and the pursuit of Happiness" must do more than occasionally pledge allegiance to the flag. It cannot be treated as a collection of meek and compliant truisms to occasionally be paraded like a prized pet. Freedom is anything but passive and submissive. It was revolutionary in 1776. It is no less today. It is also perpetually under attack and its preservation requires vigilance and hard work.

To say freedom is not "free," means more than the need for protection from outside enemies. The greatest peril often lurks within. The founders were insistent and dogged in their interpretation of freedom and democracy. They were unyielding and untiring in their endeavors to produce a constitutional structure that would inspire and harness human creativity and individual initiative (you may notice the two entrepreneurial traits). They recognized that free democracy is not a self-perpetuating machine. Once it is shaped and organized, it demands constant attention.

It is this legacy and expectation that is in our hands and on our shoulders. Lazy democracy dies. We need to recapture Franklin's wisdom that if we give up freedom for security we will not have or deserve either. Adam Smith's knowledge of supply and demand is as vital to wealth creation today as in 1776. De Tocqueville's observation regarding the importance of locally focused action needs to be rediscovered in America's political arena. Freedom to assemble, speak freely, worship according to conscience, own private property, and buy and sell remain pillars of our freedom. When this foundation crumbles, free society is dissolved and gives way to tyranny.

Democracy derives power and vitality from the right of ordinary citizens to check the checkers. Political angels and devils, sometimes less of the former and more of the latter, are found on all sides of all issues. Partisan name-calling and squabbling obscure and complicate the search for solutions. Elections do not transform winners into innocent or virtuous public officials. James Madison observed that "if men were angels, no government would be necessary." On the other hand, honesty cannot be institutionalized. Bureaucracies invite corruption and the bigger the bureaucracy the greater the opportunities for fraud. It is not institutions, but people who have received the capacity for honesty and integrity, equality and fairness, greed and vanity, and all other character traits and behaviors.

Danger threatens when centralized government grows too large and power is concentrated in fewer hands. Our forefathers put responsibility squarely on our shoulders. More directly, this is part of God's directive to subdue and have dominion over creation. De Tocqueville was gripped by the way town meetings exerted local control as an effective curb against consolidation of governmental functions and power. It is a primary reason so much authority has been delegated to the separate states. Fiscal policy is another focal point for checks and balances to maintain viable democracy. In short, the keys to long-term health and survival of American democracy and free enterprise are focused on checks and balances that foster local and smaller government, strong fiscal policy, and effective restraints to uproot and eliminate fraud and corruption.

Keynesian economic theories were introduced to combat effects of the Great Depression. They were and still today are hailed by many as almost utopian for the way they take care of average Americans. In unadorned reality, they seem to be no more than the latest form of centralized economic control that thwarts entrepreneurial behavior, the lifeblood of American free enterprise. They short-change everyone, create special-interest voting blocs, confiscate American wealth, and consolidate power for the political class. One or more groups are singled out as scapegoats. Crony-capitalism is a program of socialist economics. Bank bailouts enable banks to act as hedge fund traders. Instead of functioning as bankers, they retain profits while passing all losses back to the government that in turn are passed on to the taxpayers. When you get past the lipstick on a pig, it is still a pig. The lasting solution is less government – much less. Doing what is necessary is not pleasant or easy. It takes courage and determination.

If we want to rescue America's democracy and restore its exceptionalism, we have to return to basic entrepreneurism. It is the same behavior employed by God when creation occurred. Believe in the faith you have received and in your capacity to create. Take the actions of your convictions.

By no means are we entitled to success, but we know God is our partner and is in an everlasting relationship with each of us. Ordinary citizens have fashioned this extraordinary and great American experiment. There is no free lunch. Don't spend what you don't have. If you don't want to work, then you shouldn't eat.

Ben Carson is an African-American and Professor Emeritus of Neurosurgery at Johns Hopkins University. In a recent article, he challenged Americans to recapture the exceptionalism that has historically distinguished the United States. He recalls that ordinary citizens thrived with a "can do" attitude and hard work to conquer and transform an untamed environment into a land of incalculable success. America's accomplishments are due, in no small part, to honesty, integrity, and goodness that are evident in all endeavors of American life. He reminds us of a fundamental conclusion reached by de Tocqueville during his extended visit in the 1830's: "America is great because she is good. If America ever ceases to be good, she will cease to be great."

We dare not turn a blind eye or ear to corruption in government or business, but particularly not at a personal level. Adopting any form of national religion would be one of the worst possible things that could happen, but we must also be careful that we don't adopt a religion that worships the self-god in which every individual seeks only personal gain and control of other people.

Carson reminds us that the return to exceptionalism includes a new focus on "goodness," along with the precious freedom bequeathed in America's founding documents. In addition, we need to recommit ourselves to family values, decency, honesty, hard work, compassion, and fairness.

He ends with a hopeful note. "America can be great, but it requires real courage and conviction to resist the urge to be 'cool.' None of this means we should impose Judeo-Christian values on those who wish to adopt a different kind of lifestyle, but it does mean we should not allow an alternative lifestyle to be imposed upon us" (Carson, Ben. What Made America Great, <u>National Review Online</u>, January 7, 2014).

Freed and Re-freed for Success

Adam and Eve were the crescendo and climax of creation, the epitome of God's creativity and initiative. He modeled the entrepreneurial behavior that He anticipated from them. They received the astonishing capacity to use God's own knowledge, understanding, and wisdom as well as a wide array of resources from His storehouse. Success was assured.

Enter the serpent. The result is much worse than Antietam in 1862 or the Twin Towers in 2001. It required little flattery to deceive the first humans into thinking they could displace God. They rationalized that they could establish their own value and chose the way of the serpent. There is one problem. The prerogative of creating value rests with the Creator alone. Their self-centered act of rebellion relegated mankind to life under the tree of the knowledge of good and evil. When motivation and attitude, the vestiges of God's image, combine with lust and fear, the mixture is deadly: envy, gluttony, greed, lust, pride, sloth, and wrath. Yet, sin is sin. In a state of disconnect from the relationship with their Creator, humans are driven by motives and attitudes that focus only on self. This is the core of all sin. We imprison ourselves with desire and fear, earning only the judgment of God. For those who remain trapped in the way of the serpent, that's their life and then they die.

Those who emulate the rich fool may attain temporary gratification, but in the end they receive only permanent separation from God. What is it to be without the image of God? It is not possible to count or even think about all the blessings enjoyed because of God's image. In the end, they're all gone. No more image of God. Not ever – never. In the parable of the rich man and Lazarus, the rich man begs for Lazarus to be sent with a drop of water for relief. Separation from God is terrifying. The activity mentioned is gnashing of teeth. It is the place of ultimate regret. Denizens torture themselves that they didn't listen. It was so simple. Maybe it is the fault of someone else. It would be soothing if someone else could be blamed. It doesn't change anything. Separation from God is permanent.

Enter, actually re-enter, freedom. It is a restart. We receive re-creation because the Creator made another path by which freedom is restored. He inserted a substitute – the perfect substitute. The way of the serpent tells us it shouldn't be this way. A substitute is not supposed to be better than the A-Team player. That is embarrassing and demeaning, causing some to reject Him because of self-respect. That's not self-respect, that's self-centered arrogance.

God's grace restored the freedom stolen in the garden. We are unable to recover on our own and re-establish the relationship of the garden. Our Substitute obeyed perfectly. He lived in perfect freedom, just as the first Adam was supposed to. Then He died to complete His recovery mission.

He gives back the freedom we lost. We are no longer bound by our own chains. He also restores the interpersonal bond the Creator sought with us from the beginning. We are free, once again, to use the full measure of resources received in His image. It gets better. God gives us His Spirit and makes us His partners. We not only have access to His resources, His Spirit works with us. In fact, we work with Him to serve God and our fellowman. Being partners with an omnipotent, omniscient, and omnipresent God assures success. His partnership with us lasts through eternity. It is breathtaking and beyond powerful.

"Who shall separate us from the love of Christ? Shall trouble or hardship or persecution or famine or nakedness or danger or sword? As it is written: 'For your sake we face death all day long; we are considered as sheep to be slaughtered.' No, in all these things we are more than conquerors through Him who loved us. For I am convinced that neither death nor life, neither angels nor demons, neither the present nor the future, nor any powers, neither height nor depth, nor anything else in all creation, will be able to separate us from the love of God that is in Christ Jesus our Lord." (Romans 8:35-39 NIV)

Chapter 10

Discussion Questions:

1. How does a renewed life through the death and resurrection of Jesus change the trajectory of your life on earth?

2. "Entrepreneurial behavior wasn't discovered or invented by some clever people to establish an economic system." What are the deeper origins and implications of entrepreneurial behavior?

3. What entrepreneurial opportunities do you have personally, at home, and in your public life?

4. What major themes and insights stood out to you most in this book?

5. Now that you've read this book, what changes in faith and action are you being led to?

Epilogue

Shortly after initial completion of this manuscript, I was diagnosed with congestive heart failure with arterial blockages ranging upwards to virtually 100%. Spouse, family, doctors, nurses, and countless prayerful friends served as God's witnesses to affect His rescue and healing, though full recovery is still on the horizon. Many cards expressed wishes of well-being, but one from an auxiliary organization of our home congregation is special. It leads with the prayer of Habakkuk.

"Lord, I have heard of Your fame; I stand in awe of Your deeds, O Lord. Renew them in our day, in our time make them known; in wrath remember mercy." (Habakkuk 3:2 NIV)

So, how does this relate to entrepreneurial behavior and American Exceptionalism that we've been talking about? We know the Creator's charge: *"... subdue and have dominion..."* He has ordained us to be His partners. It is an assumption, not a choice. Remember, it is the serpent who plants an alternate wisdom: *"...ye shall be as gods..."*

As the late and long-time mentor George Beto might have said, "For crying in the rain, boy, you've received His image. What are you waiting for?!" We are to employ the Creator's knowledge, understanding, and wisdom the same way as He, to create as He creates: in the workplace and especially in the home and the community. As part of His image, we also receive motivation and attitude. The combination of motive and attitude along with His image is the very power of God. Beware, however, for that same image combined with the tree of the knowledge of good and evil can be devastating. It puts us at odds with our Creator and causes us to engage our fellowman as an object of subjugation. This ends badly, in complete and permanent separation from the Creator, where there is only *"weeping and gnashing of teeth".*

His image is not of our making or doing, but a gift – as with the one, two, and five talents received by the servants from their Master. Our creative work is done under the "cloak" of the last Adam, whose own entrepreneurial behavior carries us back into the interpersonal relationship with and intended by the Creator from the beginning, lost in the great either/or.

Our response is as simple, yet profound, as our use of His image. It is a reply of thanksgiving and joy. That's all; that's it. The Sovereign King is worshiped and adored by those He created and who just happen to also be His children and heirs. Wow! That means we receive the inheritance – already! Right Now! Still, the way of the serpent *"...prowls around like a roaring lion looking for someone to devour."* (I Peter 5:8 NIV)

Habakkuk prays for God to show His work. He leaves it to God as to how this is done. Revival is the work of God, not of man. All we can do is pray with the prophet. Of equal significance, the petition is for a revival of God's work, not ours. Too often, the serpent lures us into his false truth that it is our work that needs to be revived. Instead, we need to set our hearts and minds on God's work, vastly greater than any portion that may be claimed by us. In truth we know that we deserve only to be forgotten or worse, to be entirely unknown by the Creator.

We are wont to blame the church, except that *we are the church.* David Guzik, at his website, www.enduringword.com, advises personal revival. We are to pray for personal renewal and to inspect ourselves. Citation: ewm@enduringword.com

- Are you carrying out Jesus' directive? *"You will be my witnesses." (Acts 1:8 NIV)* Testify to what you know and see. Some overstep, believing they are not just a witness, but God's representative. Besides the arrogant and ludicrous notion that we could even come close, this is also an irresistible lure of the serpent to snatch those closest to the Creator.

- Does your conduct, especially in private where only God sees, glorify the Lord?

- Is your daily conversation profane or impure? Do you talk about Jesus with friends or ever give witness to those you have only recently met?

- Do you talk to Jesus and the Father on a regular basis, more often than when you seek His help and rescue from dire situations into which you have gotten yourself?

Habakkuk's final plea, *"in wrath remember mercy,"* recognizes the correct posture for humans. It is on our face and knees for the evil we are and do. Our only hope is mercy. It is said correctly, *"in heaven there is no justice, only mercy."*

God bless you. Be a blessing to others.
Robert G. Horn

About the Author

Robert G. Horn, Ph.D.

Now retired, Dr. Horn, an educator, worked over twenty-five years in pre-collegiate international schools in Asia and the Middle East, developing expertise in effective working relations between schools and multinational corporations. He received the Bachelor of Science from Concordia Teachers College, Seward, NE, the Master of Arts from the University of California at Santa Barbara, and the Doctor of Philosophy from Purdue University. Married to Sandra (nee) Kirch, they have two children, Christopher and Elizabeth.

Acknowledgments

Several people helped make this book a reality. The most important is the Rev. Michael Newman who served as Editor. His encouragement and active engagement were significant. Many of the ideas in the book were developed during discussion, mutual exploration and inquiry with Rev. Newman. He also formulated the study questions that conclude each chapter. I am also indebted to Dr. James Juergensen and Dr. Myra Niemeier, who read and critiqued the full manuscript. Mr. Christopher Horn and Ms. Elizabeth Cobb assisted by proofing the final manuscript. Finally, my wife, Sandra was a source of encouragement throughout the project. She also designed the cover.

RGH

20557766R00117

Made in the USA
Middletown, DE
31 May 2015